THE
rat

Also by Sandy Myhre

50 Years on Track

Scott Dixon — Indy to Indy

*Sandy Myhre gratefully acknowledges
the help and assistance of Air Tahiti Nui
and HPM New Zealand Limited*

THE rat

THE PAUL RADISICH STORY

SANDY MYHRE

HarperSports
An imprint of HarperCollins*Publishers*

National Library of New Zealand Cataloguing-in-Publication Data
Myhre, Sandy.
The rat : the Paul Radisich story / Sandy Myhre.
ISBN   978-1-86950-699-5
1. Radisich, Paul. 2. Automobile racing drivers—New Zealand—
Biography. I. Title.
796.72092—dc 22

Harper*Sports*
An imprint of HarperCollins*Publishers*

First published 2008
HarperCollins*Publishers (New Zealand) Limited*
P.O. Box 1, Auckland
Copyright © Sandy Myhre 2008

Sandy Myhre asserts the moral right to be
identified as the author of this work.

ISBN: 978 1 86950 699 5

Cover design by Gra Murdoch at Aqualuna Design
Front cover images: helmet shot courtesy of Terry Marshall,
racing car courtesy of Euan Cameron
Back cover image courtesy of Euan Cameron
Internal text design and typesetting by Springfield West

Printed by Griffin Press, Australia

100gsm UPM Fine Offset used by HarperCollins*Publishers* is a
natural, recyclable product made from wood grown in sustainable
plantation forests. The manufacturing processes conform to
the environmental regulations in the country of origin.

Contents

Acknowledgements

Just as Paul's sporting career required the help of numerous people, so too did this biography, and all those whom I approached were delighted to assist with this project. Their willingness to help is a credit to Paul's personality and demeanour, and I am enormously grateful for their time.

First up is Lorain Day and HarperCollins (New Zealand) Limited. When the contracts were signed, Lorain suggested that the petrol-heads in the office were 'dancing in the corridors'. The Paul Radisich name had that effect on them. Special thanks, too, to Kate Stone and a woman who has the best name for a book editor, Sue Page, and all the hard-working people on the design and publicity teams.

Without Frank and Robyn Radisich none of this would have been possible, and I thank them for their warm and generous hospitality. Special thanks also to Chris, Kim and Danielle for your personal memories.

Thanks to Nick Begovic, whose knowledge and insight is a marvellous motor-racing tool, and to Mary Sharp and Maureen Brennan for total support.

Without the help of Ruth Marland, my flatmate in London for six months, I wouldn't have had easy access to all the wonderful people in the UK who were involved in Paul's racing career. This also brings me to my Auckland 'flattie', Mark Dawson. Thanks mate, and I forgive you for being a South African.

David Thomson of Dunedin generously allowed me to steal worthwhile stuff from articles he had written on Paul. Allan Muir, another South Islander but now in London, provided crucial resource material from *Autosport* and pints in the local. Dave McMillan, once again, helped considerably, as did Murray Brown.

Paul's wife, Patricia, constantly took time out from being a busy mother and wife to write (very well) about her professional and personal life. She generously saved me countless hours of dogged reconstruction, for which I shall forever be grateful.

I once again acknowledge my sons Tim and Chris (Auckland) and Anthony and my daughter-in-law Caroline (France) for always and ever thinking I am capable.

To all the drivers, team managers, officials in New Zealand, Australia, Britain and the USA and the myriad other people who gave of their time to provide the silhouettes this book required, thank you time and again.

I also gratefully acknowledge the assistance of Air Tahiti Nui, and Mark Hutchinson in particular; without their help I couldn't possibly have had such a marvellous time listening to Paul's fellow competitors in Britain and Europe.

To Paul, I sincerely hope these words do justice to the time you gave me and to your life. Thank you for the honour of recording them.

Introduction

It was the beginning of winter 2007 in New Zealand and, as usual, Australian V8 Supercar rumours had been circulating for weeks. This time, however, the chitchat, the pit scuttlebutt, was far more serious than the normal whispered-behind-the-hands gossip found in any work environment. This time, the rumours had the backing of the authoritative *Australian Motorsport News*, which had raised the subject of Team Kiwi Racing's (TKR) major financial difficulties in its online edition of 29 May 2007.

Then, on 5 June 2007, a chilly Tuesday morning the day after Queen's Birthday weekend in New Zealand, came the announcement that TKR was in default of its financial obligation to the highly regarded Ford Performance Racing (FPR) organization in Melbourne. FPR had called in the lawyers and impounded the race car.

Early that same afternoon, New Zealand driver Paul Radisich issued a brief four-line press statement saying that he had resigned from Team Kiwi Racing, citing breach of contract. The team owner's official response was to metaphorically fling up his hands in martyred surprise. Paul Radisich, he announced to the media, was being 'disloyal' to the New Zealand public.

Paul politely refrained from commenting beyond his press release. In a private conversation a week or two later, he called that day 'interesting' and suggested that the retelling of it would eventually make for remarkable reading.

It undoubtedly does. But Paul Radisich has a font of stories derived from an international motor-racing career spanning more than 30 years. The machinations bouncing back and forth across the Tasman Sea on those early June days in 2007 form just a small part of the entire gamut of his chosen sport, of the life he has led.

Chapter 1

On Sunday the driver became a passenger

I was too frightened to open my eyes. I could say I saw the other side and there was nothing there, but it didn't happen like that and Jesus didn't visit me. Fortunately, the marshals did . . .

Bathurst was looking promising for Team Kiwi in 2006. Well, as good as any time in their six-year struggle to stay on the grid in the Australian V8 Supercars; maybe better, considering they'd had a third place podium finish in Shanghai the year before, which was their best result ever.

When Team Kiwi Racing was launched in 2001, many in motor racing had predicted it wouldn't survive its first year in the gladiatorial arena of Australian V8 Supercars, yet at the start of the Bathurst weekend in 2006 the team was on the cusp of acquiring the best engineering package they had ever mustered. Two days before the race, Team Kiwi Racing had signed a deal with Ford Performance Racing that would, in 2007, see a change from the familiar black Holden Commodore to a black Ford Falcon. This deal, as it turned out, was destined to have serious ramifications for all of the parties involved.

Paul Radisich was paired with young New Zealand driver Fabian Coulthard for the long-distance events of the V8 Supercar series. As his name suggests, Coulthard is related to veteran Formula 1 driver David Coulthard, who is a cousin once-removed. Fabian had come up through the New Zealand karting ranks and Formula Ford, and had won the New Zealand Grand Prix when that venerable race and trophy was downgraded to Formula Ford. In 2006, he was considered a driver on the way up, so for him to have the chance to drive with one of Australasia's top racers was good experience.

During the practice sessions TKR had been as high as 13th, but in qualifying they were 10 places lower. Still, the potential to nudge near the top 10 was ever-present, and with 161 laps of the famous circuit to play with anything could happen. Paul took the car out for the first tour of duty, and as the 50-lap mark approached his fastest time was only 0.3 seconds behind the quickest lap, which had been put down by Craig Lowndes.

As the race unfolded, it looked as though the team was ticking along reasonably well and the drivers had slotted into a rhythm. If they weren't seriously threatening the leaders, they were at least putting in consistent lap times, and in this race, of all races, consistency is a byword for success. If one or three of the frontrunners had a bad day at the office, Team Kiwi might have had a shot at the podium. Stranger things have happened at Mt Panorama.

On lap 71, Paul Radisich was at the wheel for his second stint. He brought the car into the Caltex Chase at the end of the long and fast Conrod Straight and saw there were two cars in front of him. His intention was to line this pair up at the corner and then try to slot his car on the inside of both. But nothing in motor racing is certain.

At that precise moment the two cars in front of him touched each other, which set off a chain reaction loaded with unintended consequences. The left rear wheel of the Holden Dealer Team Commodore driven by Nathan Pretty hit the right front wheel of the Team Kiwi Racing Commodore.

In an instant, the steering arm of his Commodore broke and Paul Radisich the racing driver became a thoroughly unwilling passenger. His car shot off to the left and on to an undulating grass-covered landscape. He remembers looking down because there's a drop-off to the left, and he remembers pumping the brakes because he wasn't getting any response from the steering. He remembers standing hard on the brakes, trying to do everything he could to get the car to stop, and realizing that even if he couldn't get it to stop entirely, being able to slow it down would be extremely useful. But that didn't happen.

He looked up to see the gravel trap and thought he might be able to scrub off some speed as he bounced over that. But he couldn't and by that stage he was on the edge of the grass. He thought if he could run alongside and brush up against the barrier the car would eventually come to a crunching halt. But he couldn't manage that either.

Paul was still furiously pumping the brakes, trying to slow the car down, when he saw a wall coming towards him, an earth wall filled with black tyres, a wall packed with dirt that was never going to offer him any cushioning. If all that wasn't enough, this barricade was jutting out at 90 degrees to the track. The whole event took less than 30 seconds, but to Paul it seemed like a lifetime: he knew he had a major problem.

His mind flashed back more than 15 years to his days in single-seater racing, when he was just a young racer starting out. Drivers of open-wheel cars who have any sense of self-preservation know that the best action to take before an inevitable impact is to scrunch your body up as tightly as possible and make sure you have your hands off the wheel. To this day Paul remembers doing that. He pulled his arms as far away from the steering wheel as possible, he curled his legs up as close to his body as he could. He needed to be very small indeed.

Then came the point of contact.

It was like I'd been hit in the head with a baseball bat, and it was such a massive, massive impact. The car had been going somewhere around 120 kph, so it wasn't particularly fast, but it just stopped so quickly.

I obviously passed out, but I remember the fierce impact and the fact that, when I pulled myself around, I couldn't breathe. It was so violent I thought that was the end, definitely. There was no flash of anything — just the heaviest impact you could ever imagine.

I was short of breath and I wondered if I was OK. I was struggling to breathe; I was winded and it seemed to go on for a long time, and there was a huge amount of pain around my neck and chest. My left foot had gone through the firewall and had been caught up in the pedals, but as far as that was concerned, everything felt fine at that point because there were so many other things going on.

I was hanging on, all twisted up, unable to breathe, too frightened to open my eyes and, once I was able to get my brain back into my head, the first thing that went through my mind was that I had broken my neck. Inside I was trying to feel for the seat belts and thinking I had better not touch anything. I had the presence of mind to know that if I let it go and moved I might do some more damage to myself.

All these things were running through my mind and it seemed like an age before anyone got there. It probably wasn't, it just seemed like it.

From that point I started to feel more and more pain in my left ankle. I was disoriented and didn't realize the car was on its side; all I knew was that I was twisted up and I was uncomfortable. I was in so much agony, and because of the lacerations on my neck I couldn't talk either.

What Paul didn't know at the time was that one of the first people to get to the scene of the accident was his father, Frank. He'd been watching the race from a balcony overlooking the top of the pit road and had seen a car go into the tyre wall in the distance. He wasn't sure which car it was, so he went inside the Team Kiwi garage to have a closer look on their television screen. It was then that he realized it was his son.

I tore down the stairs and saw a motorbike standing by the side of the pit garage, so I grabbed that and screamed up to the track and managed to get there before any of the rescue crews. I talked to Paul and found that he was having trouble breathing. He was pretty sore, of course, but at least he was talking to us.

Paul doesn't remember talking. He knew that something had filled up his throat and he was in agony, and he knew that not being able to talk was slowing the rescue process. The first priority for the paramedics was to get a brace around his neck, but they couldn't do that without dismantling the roof and the side pillar, because the car was lying on its side.

Paul was too frightened to open his eyes, and he knew that if he kept them tightly shut he had the best chance of keeping himself calm while the cutting gear was being used around him. He had two major concerns: he thought he might have broken his neck, and he quietly wondered whether he was about to go into shock.

After what seemed like an eternity but in reality was around 20 minutes, the Bathurst crash crews had cut away the roof and were able to get a medical harness around Paul and pull him out of the side of the car.

He was taken to the infield medical facility for examination. The track doctors knew he had a sore chest, that he had damaged his left ankle and that he was having trouble breathing, but because there are no intensive-care facilities — scanners or X-ray machines — on-site, it was decided to fly him by helicopter to Nepean Hospital in Penrith, on the outer reaches of Sydney. He needed to be out of the Bathurst environment, and, pragmatically, the race organizers needed him to go. The officials wanted to restart the race — the show needed to go on.

They gave me some morphine to take the pain away and put me in a helicopter. I knew what had happened to the car, and I was so shocked that the final impact was so hard and had been so severe. The annoying thing was that I was involved in the safety side of V8 Supercars and the area where I crashed is one that I had looked at a few times. Anything that runs between 70 and 90 degrees to the track is definitely not a good thing, and it's the ultimate irony that I thought nothing would happen. But it just shows you that it can.

At Nepean Hospital they removed the neck brace and put Paul through a full body scan, which mostly revealed the full extent of his injuries. He had very untidily broken his left foot by shattering several bones surrounding the ankle. He had lacerations to his neck and throat. The only injury that could be called 'neat', in the circumstances, was that the sternum, which runs down the centre of the chest, had snapped cleanly. At this stage, though, the doctors didn't even realize that he'd broken this particular bone.

Paul continued to have trouble breathing. When, a few hours later, the morphine started to wear off, he realized he was still suffering a great deal of pain in the chest area and he told the doctors something wasn't quite right. He was sent back to be X-rayed once more, and it was only then that the break in the sternum was discovered.

Paul's wife Patricia had been watching Bathurst from her sitting room in their home in Melbourne. She saw the black car bounce along the dirt and go hard into the barrier; she watched as the crash crews began cutting away the roof of the black Commodore; and she saw Paul being gingerly pulled out of the car in a medical harness. She made a couple of calls to the pit garage, but no one answered the telephone. She eventually got hold of their friend and former racing driver Andy McElrea, who tracked down Paul's engineer, who in turn told her that Paul wasn't responding to his radio calls.

Patricia knows the sport. She sucked in her breath and made a decision. Throwing some clothes into a bag, and packing up all the paraphernalia required for young children, she bundled up the couple's two girls, raced to the airport and boarded a plane to Sydney. When she arrived there, she pleaded with the limousine driver to take her all the way to Penrith, which is well over an hour from Sydney airport. He did, and she arrived at the emergency ward at 10.30pm Paul wasn't particularly pleased to see her or the children and even questioned why they'd come. The medical staff blamed his attitude on the morphine.

At the time of the accident, Paul's stepmother, Robyn Radisich, was at the family beach house in Cable Bay, Northland, with her grandchildren AJ and Brad. She had watched the start of the race with family friends Nick and Kaye Begovic, and then gone to her own place just down the road to watch the rest. She was following the live lap-scoring on a laptop as well as watching the race on television, and had started to feel that Paul might have a chance of 'knocking the thing off'. Then everything changed.

As the impact was shown on television, I had a strange sensation. My body felt the jolt and I got a feeling of being trapped and I couldn't move for about two minutes. But I knew he was alive, I just knew, so I didn't panic.

I managed to get hold of my son-in-law who was in the Bathurst pits, and he said they would cut Paul from the car. Then I phoned Patricia and she was in a right state organizing to fly to Sydney. She thought I should fly over, too, but even if I'd driven down to Auckland I may not have got on to a flight, and at that stage we weren't sure what hospital he'd been taken to. Patricia began texting me at every stage and I'd relay this back to the family.

Kaye Begovic stayed with Robyn for the rest of the day.

Back in Australia, the Paul Morris organization that was running the Team Kiwi car and providing the engines sent their crew chief,

Dick Smart, to the hospital. It was his first year with the team. He had come from the Honda Racing Corporation and had previously worked with Mick Doohan and Valentino Rossi in MotoGP.

The Team Kiwi Racing owner, David John, turned up at the hospital on Monday morning, and at that stage was more concerned about the patient than anything to do with the car. Paul was pumped so full of morphine that he saw everything through rose-tinted spectacles and so was, he later said, quite a bit happier to see David than he would be normally!

Frank Radisich drove to Sydney and stayed on to help Patricia with the children, and by early in the week Paul's good friend Garry Garoni had arrived on the doorstep, having flown in from the Caribbean. Garry is a very successful businessman — that he now lives in semi-retirement on a tax-haven island in the Bahamas (and one that has featured in at least one James Bond movie) is an indication of his corporate success. He realized that his mate was going to need some help and came especially to provide it. His action is a testament to the strength of their friendship.

Garry and Paul had become acquainted in 1999, when Paul was racing for Dick Johnson and Garry had just taken over as owner of Mustang boats in Australia. Paul was on the lookout for a deal and had flicked through the Yellow Pages to see what boat company might be suitable. He'd spotted the name Mustang, which appealed to him — it had that Ford ring about it, even though the two companies are totally unrelated.

When he's about to ask for sponsorship, Paul likes to start at the top, so he made an appointment to see Garry. He sauntered into his office and outlined his ideas. The sponsorship deal didn't need to be cash-based. Paul wanted a boat and he didn't really want to pay for it; he wanted to get more value out of his racing contract with the Dick Johnson team, something he knew would appeal to smart business people. The two men worked out an arrangement that saw Paul put decals on his helmet, Garry look after the boat purchase, and the birth of a mutually beneficial professional relationship. Their friendship evolved from this beginning, and has lasted a lot longer than the sponsorship deal.

As he lay immobile in his hospital bed, Paul had time to work out how his injuries had occurred. He thinks his broken sternum came from the HANS (head and neck system) device that all drivers must wear. While the sternum break was bad, the good aspect of the HANS device is that it undoubtedly saved him from breaking his neck. The lacerations on his neck must have come from the strap of his crash helmet. The ankle breaks came courtesy of the car.

The severity of the impact also affected Paul's aural senses. Even small amounts of noise bothered him considerably, and this sensation, as it turned out, would last for several months, proving to be an unpredicted and unpleasant complication to his recovery.

Paul was kept in hospital for five days, principally to establish that there were no covert medical dangers that had not manifested in the first 48 hours or so; but he was far more badly injured than the medical bulletins stated. In those early days, most people — including the majority of his fellow V8 drivers and nearly everyone in New Zealand — understood that he had a couple of broken bones. In fact, Paul was wheelchair-bound and would be for a while.

He couldn't use crutches under his arms because of his broken chest. Even if he had had the strength to hold himself up, it was too painful to do so and would have interfered with the healing process. His head couldn't tolerate noise, his ankle was useless and he was lacerated about the neck. It was in this condition that he hopped onto a plane and headed to his house in Melbourne — to a home that had just been sold.

The Victorian house he and Patricia owned had high ceilings and wide hallways, but it was loaded to the gunnels with packing boxes, which allowed little room for a wheelchair. In a couple of weeks' time they would have to vacate the premises. That was one hurdle they faced. With two young daughters in the house, the normal family noise was more than Paul's traumatized head could cope with. That was another obstacle to his recovery.

Garry Garoni stayed on for a week of nursing duty then headed back to the Caribbean, leaving Patricia with the patient. From the time he got back to Melbourne, Paul had to rely on her for everything from getting out of bed in the morning to going to bed at night, and virtually every function in between. The only things he could realistically do himself were to eat — and think.

Rightly or wrongly, every time he looked into his wife's eyes he felt he could see his own uselessness reflected back. He felt worthless, because he could see that Patricia, who is normally considered a well-oiled machine, was struggling to cope with his incapacity, which had come at a time when she needed him to be available. He found it hard to accept. In his semi-drugged state, Paul told her candidly that he didn't care about the house, the family or the consequences of moving.

Patricia couldn't understand why her husband was so remote. They'd coped with the periods of separation that the sport demands, and now, when they were forced together, he didn't seem to want to be around her. Unfortunately for them both, Paul was so dependent that he had little option but to be at home, something he really appeared to resent. Trauma can affect people in this way.

Paul Radisich was 45 years old, and these latest broken bones joined a long and formidable list that stemmed from the crazy motocross days of his youth. Admittedly, the other breaks had happened years ago and he hadn't had a serious accident since he'd moved to circuit racing at the age of 18, but even with these latest injuries he didn't think about giving up the sport. He loves it. He wanted to get well enough to get back into it as soon as he possibly could.

> *It's a different fight trying to get things back together, and when you're in that predicament your concentration span is very limited. Even to think about wanting to get to the bathroom takes all your thought and concentration. It's normal, as the body shuts down and your mind focuses on the immediate issues rather than all the other stuff.*

Paul did wonder, however, how long it would be before he could get into the new Team Kiwi Falcon. He wanted to be involved with Ford Performance Racing, and had calculated that a plaster cast is usually on for about six weeks; but he knew enough to know that the medical profession never gives any guarantees and the body takes its own time to heal. In the short term he thought it was better not to come up with any answers, but to concentrate instead on the more pressing concerns of rehabilitation.

It was just as well Paul Radisich didn't focus his attention on what he called 'other stuff', because it was all about to get tough, fraught, and at times more than a little bit nasty. He'd faced many an obstacle in the past 30 years of motor racing — but nothing quite like the winter of 2006.

Chapter 2

The children of the Western union

There were about three apple trees on the block, and at the back was an oval racetrack we had made, with a jump in it. We'd race whatever we could get in there, cars and bikes, and go round and round and round.

The Dalmatian diaspora descended on west Auckland's Henderson Valley from the early part of the 20th century. Some came fresh from the Northland region, where they had found work digging kauri gum, while others settled more directly, quick to spot that a strip of land bordered by the Waitakere Ranges on one side and an estuary on the other, and washed by the nutrients of both, was ideal for growing orchard fruit and grapes.

By the mid-1950s the majority of the 80 or so vineyards and fruit orchards out west were operated by their descendants. Walk into any one of those vineyards and ask for Ivan, and up would pop a dozen heads.

They were an independent lot, and they had to be. In those days you couldn't just call in an expert and parts for repairing equipment were not readily available, so people learned to fix anything and everything, cars included. In essence, many of the young men of the Henderson Valley who were born around the time of the Second World War — like Frank Radisich and his Croatian cousins — were the original and archetypal Westie petrol-heads long before the term came into common usage.

Frank is the son of Croatian immigrants, both his father Michael and mother Mary having emigrated from Yugoslavia in the 1920s. They met in New Zealand, married and bought a farm near Manawhai in Northland, where they remained all their working lives, eventually retiring to Avondale in Auckland. The couple had five children, three boys and two girls, of whom Frank is the third eldest.

When he was 18, Frank began competing in hill climbs in a V8 coupé, graduating three years later to a support race for the Ardmore Grand Prix in 1961. His first single-seater win came at Paritutu in New Plymouth in a Lotus 22 that he'd bought from Kenny Smith — a name that would crop up again in the life and times of the Radisich family.

By the time he was 23, Frank was spending all of his spare time in Central Motors, the service station he had established in 1960. There, he cobbled together a variety of cars to race, arguably the most exotic of which was a Matich Repco built by another Croatian called Frank, albeit an Australian. Frank Radisich raced this single-seater in the Tasman Series, helped by his brother Tony, who became something of an engineering expert on the model. Around the pits, the family set-up became known as the 'Dally Mafia'. In fact, the term referred to anyone with a Slavic-sounding surname, but most of them lived west of Auckland anyway, and all of them knew each other well — Nick Begovic, Steve Borich, Ivan Segedin and Robbie Franecivich (who later abridged his name to Francevic because it was easier to pronounce).

Frank is also remembered for introducing highly unconventional solutions to mechanical problems. He once used the extensions and universals from a socket set for the steering on a Humber 80 with a Jaguar mid-mounted engine, so if a mechanic was missing a spanner or two all he had to do was look beneath the car. There was no question that Frank could drive well, but he applied so many demon tweaks to the chassis or the engine that either one or both would give up in fright. In another life he might have been an inventor, and he has never lost his curiosity about how things work. He once totally dismantled a 'new-fangled' bag-less vacuum cleaner in the middle of a shop showroom in England.

In the early 1960s, Frank could hardly have been busier. He had married Denise Robertson in 1961, and the next year their first son, Paul, was born. A second son, Chris, arrived 18 months later, the two boys becoming third-generation New Zealanders of Croat origin. As well as starting a family, Frank had established one of Auckland's first 24-hour service stations, he was selling cars and picking up dented ones from the side of the road with his tow truck, and, as if this wasn't enough to keep him occupied, he was fitting motor racing in and around the lot. Anyone living close to

Central Motors couldn't help but hear Frank's racing cars on the dyno, or see him testing a low-slung single-seater on the roads. There was no such thing as a decibel limit in those days, and the police, who knew what he was up to, were more likely to want to have a look than book him. It speaks volumes for the times.

Denise was just 18 years old when she married Frank. She was genteel, but she had come from what would today be described as a dysfunctional family, and so Frank of necessity had to take over much of the day-to-day care of their two little boys. Wherever he went they tagged along — at home, at the service station, at the race track. Today, if there is any lasting legacy of his birth mother's problems, it is Paul's abstemious attitude towards alcohol consumption.

Perhaps inevitably the marriage disintegrated, and along came the diminutive Robyn. With two daughters to support, she had trotted off to Central Motors to pump gas, and, as it turned out, to meet Frank. However, the timing of their togetherness didn't quite conform to what society considered correct and proper, even in the 'sixties era, when it was all about making love, not war.

Robyn cared for her two girls and Frank's two boys in her little flat in Edmonton Road, which of course was convenient but also a way of getting everyone better acquainted. At this time, Paul, the eldest, was 11 years old and Chris was about 9. Robyn's girls, Kim and Danielle, were even younger. They'd crank up the stereo, pop on the vinyl 45s or LPs, and dance on the coffee table to 'Rockin' Robin' or 'Jet' or 'Rock Around the Clock' and everything from Elvis.

They were old enough to know that there were family secrets

swirling around, and because of this the children grew close more quickly than they otherwise might have. Then again, kids are kids. The boys had their motocross and had no intention of letting anything stand in the way of that.

By 1974, Robyn and Frank Radisich had officially begun their life together and Paul remembers a big white van turning up at the house.

The girls and Robyn were all quite flighty, here one minute and gone the next. When they first moved in, it would only last about two days and then Robyn and Frank would have an argument and they'd be getting the van back. Robyn and the girls would be gone for a week, then they'd come back and stay for a week and then go again. It was hilarious, and Chris and I used to have bets with each other over how long they would last. We probably didn't help the process, because half the arguments were about the girls not getting on with the boys or the other way around. After about 18 months, there was no more moving out.

In a highly unusual move for the 'seventies, and against the advice of his friends, Frank fought for, and won, custody of Paul and Chris. At such a young age they may not have understood the semantics of a messy divorce, but Chris says they knew enough not to want to give up the closeness to their father: 'We really wanted to live with Dad more, because of the life we had and didn't want to lose, as we knew life with our mother would be very different and we would not get to do all the things we wanted to.'

The primary agents uniting the two families were unquestionably the service station and motor racing. Robyn's father, Bob Cole, had been heavily involved in speedway, so she and the girls weren't being introduced to anything new in that department. Nonetheless, the joining of the two households meant that there were enormous adjustments to be made, and everything had to fit in alongside work at the service station, circuit racing for Frank, and motocross for the boys. In the middle of all this turmoil, Frank's Croatian-born parents moved in.

'I'll never forget Grandma,' says Danielle. 'As far as she was concerned, everything was for Frank and the boys and she'd go around the house giving the Sign of the Devil to Kim and me. She felt women had a certain role to play in a household and we obviously did not fulfil this in her eyes.'

Today, they would be called a 'reconstituted family'. Back then, they considered themselves to be like television's *The Brady Bunch*, but the reality was that there were a lot more tears and tantrums. Paul was the tidy freak and the one who didn't eat a vegetable until he was 18. Chris was studious, the brains of the family, with a bedroom that smelled like a panel-beater's shop because he was always painting slot cars. Kim was outgoing like Paul, while Danielle seemed more like the quiet Chris.

They all loved *The Secret Life of Edgar Briggs*, the TV show about a hapless espionage agent played by David Jason, and when they couldn't see it on the television they'd use an old recorder to tape the soundtrack and then they'd sit around and laugh at the programme without the pictures. It kept them amused for hours.

The boys went to Pomaria Road Primary School and to Liston College, which was run by the Christian Brothers and where Paul was one of the 30 foundation pupils. He's amazed he was accepted at the staunch Catholic school, because he'd never been to church. However, he thinks Frank may have offered to fix the priests' cars or buy a wing of a school that had yet to be built in order to get them enrolled. Kim and Danielle went to Sunnyvale Primary, Henderson Intermediate School, and Waitakere College. Danielle had 'behavioural issues' and didn't exactly conform to the standards of Waitakere College, so she was 'invited' to attend St Dominic's College.

The Radisich home in Sturgess Road sat on half an acre that featured a few motocross jumps in between a couple of apple trees. Eventually, Paul and Chris built their own extended race course. The layout was a lap of the yard, through the garage, up the long driveway, across the road, down to the railway station and back again. At the Henderson rail siding, they cleared some gorse and set up another track so that they could ride every day, pretending to be Ivan Mauger and sliding around speedway style. It was difficult to do in the dry, recalls Chris, but it was great fun in the wet, even if they had to extract the gorse prickles out of their backsides at the end of the day.

There were larger blocks nearby owned by other Dalmatians. The boys would push their little motorbikes on the footpath to the Golden Sunset vineyard, and when they were certain there were no cops around they'd crank up the motor, hop on and ride.

They learned to drive tractors so that they could smooth out the ruts and move the dirt around to make jumps between the vines. Although the owner, Vic Talyansich, seemed nonplussed about these kids tearing up his property, he left them to it — perhaps from an ulterior motive: the lawn-mower engines that powered the bikes screamed so loudly that they kept the birds away. However, they weren't the first kids to do this sort of thing; Nick Begovic says there was already an established precedent:

> *Robbie Francevic and I and others used to tear around the Babich vineyard in Ranui. We made a hill-climb track and would run up and down, and about 40 years later Paul and his mates were doing exactly the same thing at Steve Pecard's vineyard and other places.*

The boys progressed to the cars that Frank brought home from the yard — and to their mother's Mini, which for several years was the only car in which Chris could reach the pedals. He had his first accident in the square little British car when he banged it into the garage door. He was five years old.

There were a few more scratches to vehicles along the way, and Paul inflicted the worst one. He loaded Frank's Torana XU1 with a few friends from school and went to the vineyard to thrash around and show off. He ploughed into a tree. Chris wonders how they didn't kill themselves before they were 15, but they all scraped through, and amazingly none of them got so much as a speeding ticket until many years later.

After the two families had merged, the bulk of the day-today childcare fell to Robyn, but, as Central Motors grew and she became more involved in the business, nannies entered the picture. One was so fat that she broke the bathroom scales when she stood on them, and it didn't take long for the kids to realize she was having a rollicking affair with the driving instructor. Another was so old she simply couldn't control them, a situation they mercilessly exploited.

Possibly out of necessity and probably as good training, Frank and Robyn took the children along to work at the petrol station after school and in the holidays. They learned to pump petrol and sell car parts, and during the busiest time on Saturday night when *The Eight O'Clock* newspaper came out, they worked hard purveying the paper, chocolates, lollies and party ice. Always a pioneer, Frank had come up with the idea of using the service station to sell groceries, mainly to cater for night-shift workers in the area.

There were occasional customers who didn't want to be served by baby-faced kids on the grounds that they didn't know enough about things like spark plugs. In fact, the kids normally knew more than most of those who were doing the asking. They were all well aware that Frank and Robyn used employment as a clever way of keeping an eye on them, but it kept them together as a family and there was precious little choice.

Even celebrating Christmas was limited. They'd get two hours off work for lunch, which alternated between Nana Jacobs (Robyn's mother) and Nana Cheak (Robyn's ex-husband's mother, who called Paul her grandson and followed his career avidly until the day she died). Kim says that when she became a parent herself it took a while for her to relax enough to enjoy Christmas Day, because she felt a lingering guilt at having more than an hour or two off work. On New Year's Eve, it wasn't much different. They would all work until midnight, when Robyn would bring out the bubbly. After that they'd all be so tired they'd go home.

With Frank so involved in single-seater racing, it might be natural to expect that he would like his boys to follow, and so get them involved through the classic precursor classes of karts and Formula Ford. He didn't push them down this route, though, and to this day people ask him why Paul and Chris were both into bikes and not cars. The answer is decidedly pragmatic:

> *A motocross track has something like a hundred bends, and they have to be learned within five laps or so. Now, if you look at Paul's record he's always been able to establish a good time on a new track, and I put that down to his early years. And karts in those days weren't quite so sophisticated, they were junk really; and there weren't many tracks, but motocross was strong. I thought — I damn well knew — it could relate to car driving. There is no difference, you get the feel.*

Paul certainly didn't know anything different. He accepted the advice of his father, and by the time he was 10 years old he was dominating the Senior 125cc class and seeded in the top 10. When he moved on to the bigger 250cc class, he was once again seeded in the top five. At 16 years of age he represented his country at the Australasian finals in Tahiti at an international meeting, along with other prominent motocross riders of the time, such as Terry Meaks, Rex Avery and Russell Maiden.

However, he very nearly didn't make it there. A strike by Air New Zealand had restricted cargo space, and Frank was convinced that the bikes would be stranded, leaving Paul unable to compete. Ever-resourceful, Frank dismantled the 125 Kawasaki so that every part, including the engine, could go on as hand luggage. It set off the security alarms, but somehow he talked the airline staff into allowing him to lug the stuff on board, although they did warn him not to put the bags in the overhead locker for safety reasons. He couldn't have lifted them anyway.

The event was held over two weekends, and was won by a young American called Ricky Johnson, who went on to become a superstar in the sport. Paul can't quite remember where he finished in the series — somewhere in the top five or six, he thinks — but he does recall the dusky Tahitian maidens who could sing in English but couldn't speak it. Not that at that time he was exactly socially innocent. He'd been seeing a good Catholic girl from Henderson for some time, and she used to shinny up the drainpipe to his bedroom for regular nocturnal visits.

Paul had left school at 15 to become a mechanical apprentice at Central Motors Service Centre, and although he'd applied himself — because it's in his nature to complete things — his heart really wasn't in fixing other people's cars. In fact, he thought he was useless because most of his attention had gone into motorbikes. He was supposed to go to night school twice every week, but he and another apprentice mechanic (Graeme Sorenson) skipped a month of classes to go to speedway practice and then out for a beer, because they thought that was more important. When the foreman, John Moses, found out they were skiving off, he put the pair on tea-making and sweeping duty, and any other boring task on offer. They never skipped another night-school session again.

Paul's attitude to work — an activity that filled in the time between motocross events — probably arose because he was good at his sport. His sporting focus gained an additional incentive as time progressed, and as his riding started to attract wider public attention.

At 18 years old, Paul headed to Western Springs for the inaugural indoor stadium motocross event, a venue where he wanted to make his mark. He did. In one of the heats he mistimed a double jump, was hurled off the bike, landed on his head and ended up in hospital with a compression fracture of his spine. It was two months before he could stand upright again. In 10 years in motocross, he had broken two collarbones, a knee, an ankle and an arm; hardly surprisingly, it occurred to him that there must be an easier way to go motor racing. He decided to approach his dad to talk circuit racing.

'Frank tried to make up every excuse why I shouldn't do it, and we had much discussion about it, but at the end of the day he could see I was keen to get involved with the cars, so he said he'd help as much as he could. I think underneath he was quite happy about it.'

It's easy to know which way Paul's thoughts were heading. Basically, it was to wherever his father thought they should head, and that was dictated by budget. However, by this stage Paul had a large poster of Formula 1 driver Graham Hill in his bedroom . . . because he thought it was 'cool'. He'd acquired the poster when Frank had sold an automotive accessory shop called Track and Street, and he particularly liked the helmet design. It wasn't the nouveau, design-house, structured, artistic piece drivers have today, but somehow this poster kindled his teenage imagination. He used to stare at it a lot.

There were a number of starting options in single-seaters (Formula Vee or Formula Ford), and there was saloon-car racing, which at that time was in a healthy position with a strong manufacturer-supported championship. Ford, Toyota, Holden, Fiat and Chrysler took the Benson & Hedges Series very seriously, specifically preparing works cars and hiring only those drivers they considered to be capable of winning outright. The rest of the grid was made up by car dealers driving their own brands and competing under the 'drive on Sunday, sell on Monday' philosophy — or so they told the boss.

Compared with some of the other options, saloon-car racing wasn't very expensive, and this, coupled with the fact that numerous family members were already competing in this type of motor sport, meant that the series was ready-made for the Radisich boys. Paul was 17 and Chris was 15. They borrowed Robyn's Mazda 323 without asking her, and entered the long-distance 500-mile event at Pukekohe. Chris slipped out of school early and went with Paul to the track, where the officials turned

37

a blind eye to these kids being together in the car. After all, these particular kids probably knew more about car control than a considerable number of the once-a-year competitors out there.

The Radisich boys placed fifth in the small-car class in their first event, took the roll cage out, and handed the Mazda back to their stepmother. They had been beaten by Robyn and their father in a Mini GT in a race that Robyn says was filled with 'real' racing drivers — and her. She's doing herself a disservice: Robyn and Frank's fourth outright afforded her the highest placing ever for a woman in the event.

Paul, meanwhile, had caught the motor-racing bug, and a year later he teamed with his father in a Toyota Trueno 1600cc for an attack on the entire three-race series. The first stop was the sprint event at the tight Bay Park track with its uneven camber. There were high hopes for a win, provided the weather stayed dry. It didn't, and on totally unsuitable tyres they finished fifth again. The second event, at Manfeild, was promoted by the circuit founders Rob and Wendy Lester, who were well-known in Manawatu and indeed in New Zealand motor-racing circles.

None of the pundits there that day counted on the driving ability of the teenager from Henderson, and from the start of the race this upstart scrap of a kid in a tiny Toyota snapped at the heels of Leo Leonard, one of New Zealand's most successful and experienced racers, who was driving a V8 Falcon specifically prepared for the event. No matter what he did, Leo couldn't seem to shake off this annoying little car behind him, and it began to look like Paul Radisich might actually win the race.

For the want of a few pints of petrol, he might have. When he came in for his final pit stop, the fuel churn meant for the team's Mini was used on his car instead, and, with about 10 laps of the race to go, when he was about to pass Leo Leonard for the lead, Paul ran out of fuel. He coasted into the pits and the team put in a splash of gas to get him home in third place: 'The Toyota was stressed to say the least, but that was the start of thinking that maybe there is something there, because I knew I could have beaten Leo Leonard.'

Such was the impression he made, that to this day no one can remember who got second. In the final round at Pukekohe, Paul ran as high as third until the car was retired with engine trouble near the end of the race.

What he needed was something bigger. What he got was something smaller, much lower to the ground, and so very much more powerful.

Chapter 3

The race must go on

Suddenly an opportunity presented to get out and drive a single-seater, it was surreal. At that stage I don't know if I was interested in single-seaters, to be honest, but from that day onwards I realized how precise a real car can feel.

At the start of the 1980s, New Zealand began to enjoy the freedom afforded by the economic reforms of Rogernomics, and motor racing, that most expensive of sports, was attracting a portion of the *nouveau riche* to its ranks. Some of them could drive passably well. Others merely thought they could.

By this time, single-seaters had moved from the brutish Formula 5000s to the more nimble Formula Pacific class (known elsewhere as Formula Atlantic), and some of the drivers who competed Down Under went on to enjoy illustrious recognition. For example, Finnish driver Keke Rosberg won the Stuyvesant Series in 1977 and became World Formula 1 champion in 1982, while Danny Sullivan and Bobby Rahal (both Americans) won the Indianapolis 500 post-Aotearoa. Visitors like these viewed a trip to New Zealand as an opportunity to acquire additional competitive miles during the northern winter off-season, in order to return, so the theory went, more on top of the game than if they'd stayed at home in the snow. Many of them were surprised at the furious pace of the racing here.

Out in the western suburbs of Auckland at this time was a second-generation Dane, Garry Pedersen, who was a business and racing contemporary of Frank Radisich. Garry and Frank's kids knew each other as well. Paul would drop by the Pedersen house to chat with Garry's son, Mark, about his karting and to give him parts to help out. Looking back today, Garry says Paul was probably there to see Louise Pedersen as much, if not more, than Mark or the parents.

Also close to the Pedersen family was Dave McMillan, who as a race mechanic had gone to England with New Zealand driver Graeme Lawrence to work on his Formula 2 McLaren. He had also worked with race engineer and team owner Fred Opert in the United States and Canada, before coming home to race and to win the Formula Ford championship in 1973. He moved to a Ralt RT1 to start his serious single-seater assault in the premier division, before acquiring the newer RT4, and both of these Ralts were prepared in Garry's garage in Glen Eden.

Most of the Ralts had Ford engines, but Nissan Motor Company was keen to install one of their Japanese power plants into one as a test bed, and so two of these engines were delivered to Garry Pedersen's garage.

'The Nissan was a bigger four-valve, 1600 engine, and lower to the ground but not as small as the Ford. No one else wanted to do it, so we took it on as a challenge,' Garry says simply.

Mark Sheehan (universally known as Jandals), Dave McMillan and Garry took the RT1 chassis and the Nissan engine into Auckland city on the back of a trailer and cobbled the package together in the basement of Citizen Watches, which was one of Dave's sponsors.

New Zealand champion racer David Oxton was the first to drive it, and the RT1 Nissan immediately went surprisingly well, which they hadn't expected. Its race availability depended on which Ralt Dave McMillan wanted to drive. In the end he chose the RT4 with the Ford engine, because it was better tested and because of his existing Ford connections. This freed up the RT1. Garry Pedersen remembered 'the kid up the road', and within a week Paul Radisich was in the driver's seat for the most prestigious event of the year: the New Zealand International Grand Prix.

In the circumstances, it was quite remarkable. Paul Radisich had only ever competed in three saloon-car races prior to this, and he was being plonked into a vastly different and infinitely faster and superior single-seater. At just 19 years old, he was preparing to dice with the well-established and highly experienced men of single-seater racing — like Graeme Lawrence, Dave McMillan, Kenny Smith and Dave Oxton — in the most competitive New Zealand series of the day, and he attracted a great deal of media attention.

In testing, Paul adopted a cautious approach and took about 100 laps to get his time down to under a minute, the result being that more than one person in the pits privately thought he was far too young. Paul might have shown some speed in a car with a roof over his head, but that hardly qualified him to race a single-seater, let alone one with wings and slick tyres. In essence, he had to prove that he was as good as his supporters suggested.

Paul, on the other hand, was prepared to capitalize on what was presented to him, but he'd been competing since he was seven, and in a sense this was just another competitive outing. At that point he would have lacked circuit race-craft no matter what he was driving.

Being in the Atlantic car certainly sped up the learning process, and from that day onwards I decided that was the path I wanted to take in motor racing, so there were a lot of things crystallized out of that.

There was, however, a bit of a problem.

All that testing took its toll on the engine: it ran the bearings and no one could get any parts for it, although God knows they tried. The night before the New Zealand Grand Prix, Nissan's PR manager, Bob Penman, telephoned all his contacts in the entire organization, while Frank phoned every other person in the world, but by night's end they were no further ahead than they had been in the afternoon. They hadn't acquired a single part for the car. The kid driver wasn't going anywhere.

It was the most frustrating start (or lack of it) one could possibly have to a fledgling international motor sport career. From being on such a high after qualifying for his first single-seater event, and at that a Grand Prix on the technically demanding and very fast Pukekohe circuit, surrounded by the most able and most experienced drivers of the day, lapping up the media attention, and with crowds waiting in the grandstand to see how he performed, he didn't. He was stuck in the paddock and forced to watch a race he could only now dream about. The sole palliative to the whole affair was that the New Zealand International Grand Prix of 1981 was won by his mentor, Dave McMillan.

So with the Nissan-engined Ralt sitting forlornly in the garage without the required parts, the family came up with another plan to contest the remaining three rounds in the international series and give Paul much-needed experience before the winter layoff. They passed the hat around a coterie of Croats to buy the Ralt RT4 chassis owned by Mike Rosen, the son of a wealthy California Jewish couple. Mike had come to New Zealand to drive for Dave McMillan in the international series and had left the car here. Shortly afterwards he died from a drug overdose in a motel in Fiji, and in the confusion that followed it appears that the Radisich cheque got lost in the mêlée. To this day Paul isn't sure whether the car was properly paid for.

The other problem was the chassis didn't have an engine, so a standard-kit Ford BDA engine had to be flown in from England. This was arranged by the Halliday brothers, who were importing Cosworths at the time. (These brothers are probably better known today for being the father and uncle of New Zealand A1GP and Champcar racer, Matt Halliday.) Frank built the engine up, but without any of the modifications of virtually all the other Formula Pacific engines, and in the frenetic rush to get everything done there was no time for testing. Even so, Paul acquitted himself well at Manfeild and Pukekohe in his first two serious races, coming home fifth in both events. The next race was at Bay Park.

In theory, Paul now had a bit of experience, but not much. Two races don't make an expert, but in the main race at the Mt Maunganui circuit, and to the astonishment of hundreds, he led for a good portion of the race, only to eventually succumb to reigning champion David Oxton. He had beaten everyone else in the field in only his third single-seater race: a classic case of impetuous youth clashing with the experience and ability of men far older and wiser — and emerging triumphant.

There are two sides to every story, however, and if you talk to Kenny Smith about that day, he has another viewpoint entirely:

> *Paul kept banging into me, putting his nose cone on mine. After the race I was so incensed I got out of the car and went to punch him, but I couldn't because he had his helmet on. So I hit him in the chest and told him I'd kill him. He ran back into the pits, probably thinking I was this mad bastard, but he'd insulted me.*

In a television interview immediately after the race, Paul Radisich suggested that it was time for the 'old' men of the sport to make way for the new brigade, which hardly endeared him to those he was trying to beat. With the confidence of youth, he simply didn't understand that Kenny and most of the other 'oldies' in the race were highly capable of giving him a lesson in racing protocol. To be fair, though, Paul had been 'encouraged' by his sponsor to stand up for himself. Tony Ward, the owner of Scrubbers Bathrooms, worked on the theory that all publicity is good publicity.

*Tony is a terrific guy and he was a big help, and he
kept on saying, 'You have to cause some controversy.
Look at Kenny Smith, bloody old geriatric, you've got
to get in there and wind them up.' He was feeding
me what I should be saying and it worked! I got some
exposure.*

Like his driving, Paul very quickly learned a thing or two about
dealing with the public (and his fellow competitors), and thereafter
adopted what many in motor sport call the 'Peter Brock attitude',
to become the model racing citizen. He learned to keep his mouth
shut and, according to Kenny Smith, the principal protagonist in
this saga, Paul grew from being 'a smart-arse little shit' to a driver
who eventually provided him with some of the best dices he's
had in his long career. Since that day at Bay Park, Kenny says
Paul has always been a gentleman.

The family thought the world of him no matter what. They
stuck together through thick and thin — from motocross to
saloon cars and into single-seaters — travelling throughout New
Zealand in the interest of the sport and of Paul, crammed into
whatever car Frank had available at the time. Four kids, two
adults, a mass of racing paraphernalia, and a journey that could
take all day is no mean undertaking, and to while away the
time the younger kids adopted diversionary tactics. They'd guess
the make and model of approaching cars, they'd play 'corners'
(squashing the kid on the left side for a left corner and vice
versa), and they'd make up their own songs, such as this one
(the tune is unknown):

The Radisich Mazda it went round the track going
Brooom brooom brooom brooom *all the day,*
Frank got so ambitious he blew off Ken Smith,
Now you should hear Ken say,
'Oh my car, oh my car,
What a sad day when I lost it . . .'

Their favourite destination was Bay Park Raceway in Mt Maunganui, because they could stay at the 'in' hotel of the seventies, Willow Park in Tauranga, and order breakfast from room service. When they got to the track they'd run around it, which was a legacy from their motocross days. Today, they all wish they could still do it.

At the end of Paul's three single-seater races and with the media considering him something of a young tyro, the family decided he should head across the Tasman Sea to contest Australia's top single-seater category and acquire all-important experience. He would become a professional racing driver, with his own team contesting an international series outside New Zealand. At least, that was what it looked like on the surface.

They bought an old Transit van, fitted it with wooden slats in the back, put in all the spares, added an unlicensed trailer, loaded the Ralt RT4 onto that, and put the lot on a boat and headed across the Tasman Sea. They called it 'Grizzwells on Tour' and decided that Papa and Mama Bear would fly over for the racing.

Many a New Zealander had, of course, competed in Australia

in the Tasman Series, but few considered the Australian segment as a stepping-stone to international stardom. In any case, the Tasman Series was defunct as a dual-country competition, as both countries were running their own domestic series for Formula Atlantic autonomously. Some drivers competed in events in both series, but any driver with serious ambition headed to Europe. In consciously choosing to go to Australia, Paul was inadvertently setting a precedent; but it wasn't his intention — the reality was he didn't have the budget to attempt racing further afield.

Paul went with Graeme Sorenson, the apprentice from Central Motors with whom he had skived off night school. Graeme didn't have very much more experience at being a race mechanic than Paul had at being a racing driver, but that didn't enter the equation. They were mates, setting off for a nine-month odyssey, running away from home with Mum and Dad's blessing and money, with weekend racing thrown in for good measure.

In Australia in 1981, the National Panasonic Formula Pacific championship had been introduced and immediately became the country's top single-seater category. Even in the first season it had produced close and exciting racing, but more importantly perhaps, the grid was filled with emerging young talent keen to establish ascendancy — people like John Smith, Alfredo Costanzo, John Bowe, Andrew Miedecke and Charlie O'Brien. The Aussie drivers, with their big transporters and their teams of mechanics, laughed at the young Kiwis doing it out of a Transit van that they slept in when they couldn't afford even a flea-pit motel. Paul didn't care; he was racing and, as the Aussies were to find out, he was learning.

I remember at Lakeside in Queensland there was a yellow flag at the top of the hill and all these guys acknowledged the yellow by raising their arms, and since I was the only one who lifted off the throttle I lost a huge amount of ground. That was a lesson for sure, but most of the time I would just basically tag along at the back of the pack anyway.

He didn't stay dawdling for long. He was third at Sandown and began to earn racing respect from competitors and spectators. That's quite something, considering the company he was keeping. For instance, at the Australian Grand Prix at Calder Park in November 1982, Paul's fellow competitors included Alain Prost, Jacques Lafitte and Roberto Moreno, who filled the finishing grid in that order. Paul was 16th.

He and Graeme had a few laughs during the year, and along the way Paul developed as a competitor, but when it came time to ship all the racing paraphernalia back home they looked every inch the country bumpkins. There was no warrant for the car or the trailer, nor were either of them registered; the boys didn't even have their licences with them. When the 'Grizzwells' came to the attention of the wharf police, they could produce nothing to show that their 'professional' racing team enjoyed any sense of legitimacy. The border police were so appalled that they told the small flock of Kiwis to go back to where they'd come from, or words to that effect.

As Paul had acquired some experience and had proved himself in several races, the family decided he should go back to Australia the following year, 1983, to contest the Australian Drivers Gold Star Series. This time, though, they employed a professional to run the team. They sought the services of Graham Watson, a fellow New Zealander with the stature of a jockey. He was a former racer who had switched to team ownership and who was based in Sydney. Over the years, 'Wattie' has had a successful list of seriously good drivers emerge from his camp, including Mark Webber, Scott Dixon, Nelson Piquet, Roberto Moreno, Keke Rosberg and David Brabham. He is still Jonny Reid's manager.

The car of choice for Paul was a Ralt RT4 Formula Pacific, and once again he was competing against international drivers of serious calibre. The Australian Grand Prix at Calder Raceway, for example (which was the final round in the series), featured Roberto Moreno (Brazil), Jacques Lafitte (France), Josele Garza (Mexico), and Allen Berg (Canada). There were also a number of Australians in the line-up, including Geoffrey Brabham, and a man who went on to win a World Formula 1 title, Alan Jones.

At this Grand Prix race, Paul stalled in the warm-up lap and the marshals had to push-start him. Unfortunately, when they did this they inadvertently broke the wing mount on the back of the car. With a few laps to go, the wing came off completely, but amazingly, even without it, he managed to finish seventh and beat fellow Kiwis David Oxton and Brett Riley in the process. He ultimately finished fourth in the championship, which was won by Alfredo Costanzo.

Off the track, Paul was learning about other aspects of life as a racing driver. Whereas in the past his racing had been very family focused, this season his team was more independent, although there were normally one or two family members at every race. It took a bit of adjustment on all sides. Wattie has never been keen on what he sees as interference from the relatives of racing drivers, even if they are paying the bills. He thought Paul was a 'great guy', but he wasn't exactly enamoured with Frank and others poking their noses in. Families, he muttered, can be a pain, but that wasn't the end of it.

At the end of the season there was a disagreement about who owned and owed what. Frank would phone, but Wattie wasn't answering calls. The race car and some of the equipment was stored in a local garage. Someone (and, although there are suspicions, no one is prepared to name names) broke into the lock-up, pushed the car onto a trailer and simply towed it away. The tabloid media got hold of the saga and a picture of a full-bearded Frank wearing a 'Tahiti 79' T-shirt was splashed on the front pages. Eventually a judge made sure the right people got the correct bits back. It was unpleasant at the time, but no hard feelings remain, and today Wattie and Frank talk quite often.

With two Australian seasons under his belt, Paul's next concern was what he would do for an encore. Any Down Under racing driver with ambition who wanted to prove his worth had to go further afield, and that, of course, meant spending more money. The New Zealand Driver to Europe scheme was nominally still in existence, but the award was either a plane ticket and a handshake for good luck or a loan that had to be repaid. Paul Radisich was clearly the next best candidate for the scholarship, but it did not and could not buy him a drive.

A season in the British Formula 3 championship was the ideal starting point for the next phase of his career, since so many drivers from this essentially 'junior' formula had gone on to compete in the premier Formula 1. There were several New Zealanders doing well in England as mechanics and team owners in this category — surely that would mean that a Kiwi driver would have a foot in the door, or at the very least get sympathetic hearing from the team owner. Well, that was the somewhat naïve view of New Zealanders back home.

The bald fact was that the series would cost £100,000. The equation was simple: if you had the money, you had a spot; if you didn't have the cash, then there wasn't a spot available. Team Radisich would have to raise the money through their sponsorship department — which consisted of Frank and Paul. Worse still, they had only four months in which to achieve this: from the end of the Australian season to the start of the 1984 Formula 3 series in Britain.

Paul contacted Denny Hulme, one of the outstanding beneficiaries of the Driver to Europe scheme a generation beforehand, and a man who had become Formula 1 World Champion in 1967. He had retired from the world stage in 1974, but he continued to contest saloon-car events closer to home. If you asked him what he did for a living, he'd tell you he was 'scratching around' in his house on Lake Rotoiti.

Denny was really good. I went to his place and he took me to the hot springs. We had a good chat and he told me about his experiences one-on-one, and it was amazing. It was the first time I had had anything to do with him — prior to that he would just grunt — and he was always ready to give away advice.

Paul and his backers hooked into a national lottery that was being run by the police to raise money for charity and which offered houses, boats and cars for the winners. He was featured on some of the tickets as 'Racing for New Zealand' and the intention was that a percentage of the ticket price would be allocated to his cause. That was the first step.

Motorsport New Zealand had allowed them to quote the Driver to Europe scheme, so they nominally had the blessing of the governing body for the fundraising scheme. Armed with these two elements, Denny and Paul headed to the Beehive in Wellington to talk with the Labour Government's Minister of Sport, Mike Moore, who provided them with a list of companies in New Zealand that were exporting to the United Kingdom.

'It wasn't enough to get us there in total, but it was great for a young guy to get Denny behind things and be prepared to help,' Paul said at the time.

He was on the journey.

Chapter 4

Here, there and everywhere

I didn't have a bean. I was 24 and trying to make a go of it. I felt pretty isolated, there was only me, alone, and what should have been the happiest of days unfortunately were not.

Based on the promise of some money from the new national lottery, Paul Radisich had, ostensibly, start-up funds for England, so he left behind a humid Auckland summer in 1984 and travelled north, arriving in London in the middle of the English winter. A deal organized through Richard Elliott of Continental Airlines helped enormously: Paul didn't have to pay full fare — although it did mean he had to stop at all stations.

On one journey to the UK, we stopped in California and went from there to Houston. In Houston, the airline requested volunteer passengers to give up their seat to London, since they were overbooked. The incentive was meal vouchers, free overnight accommodation and some cash in the hand. I didn't need to be asked twice. All my Christmasses had come at once!'

In England, he joined a team based at the famous Northampton track of Silverstone and headed by Murray Taylor, a former motor-sport correspondent for the *Christchurch Star*. None of the actual money had eventuated when Paul first approached Murray about racing for the team, but Murray courageously took a punt, anticipating that he'd get the funds at some stage in the future. He was a Kiwi, after all, and 'Racing for New Zealand' appealed to him.

Murray was immersed in motor racing in England, first as a press officer for the Royal Automobile Club (the RAC is still the governing body for motor sport), then as a correspondent for *Motoring News* and *Motor Sport*, covering Formula 2; trekking around Europe to go to motor racing and getting paid for it, is how he describes it.

He had brought American driver Danny Sullivan to New Zealand in 1977 (when Keke Rosberg won the championship), and Italian Teo Fabi the following year. He'd also run a couple of drivers who had graduated from the rough-and-tumble world of Formula 3 to Formula 1 — Ricardo Patrese from France and Alan Jones of Australia. His stable had included the highly talented New Zealand-born Mike Thackwell, whom we like to claim as our own even if he did move to Australia with his parents at about the age of seven.

The team that Paul was to join was no back-runner. In the previous season they had run Irishman Kenny Acheson in a March, and they were leading the series halfway through the season. They were up against the team run by Ron Dennis, who now heads McLaren Racing International, and his driver, Stefan Johansson, who is now Scott Dixon's manager. At the series midpoint, Ron said to Murray that he should enjoy the season 'while he could'. Ron dumped the March they'd been using and bought a Ralt from New Zealander Rob Wilson. (The New Zealand connection went further still, the chief engineer being Dunedin man Dick Bennetts.) The mid-season move paid off for Dennis: driving the Ralt, Stefan Johansson won the series by one point over Acheson.

As well as engineering for Ron Dennis's team, Dick Bennetts had set up his own Formula 3 team in 1981, starting with Jonathan Palmer. The year before Paul Radisich arrived in England, Bennetts ran a young Brazilian driver by the name of Ayrton Senna da Silva. Eventually, 13 of his former drivers made the grade to Formula 1, which demonstrates why every young and promising driver wanted to race in that championship. This was the heady world of British Formula 3.

Paul was part of a three-car team that included Andrew Gilbert-Scott (who is now Juan Pablo Montoya's manager) and Swiss driver Mario Hayten. Paul's mechanic was Englishman Paul Thompson, but, like every Kiwi driver who had headed away overseas before, Paul thought it normal to pick up some tools and start tinkering anyway. 'I'd go into the workshop and if there was talk of changing the ratios, I'd grab a set of spanners and start to do it myself. It caused quite a bit of ruckus and I was told to clear off.'

For the first time in his racing life, Paul was essentially on his own. All of the jobs he'd been used to being involved with — like preparing the car and organizing the team — were now being done by someone else. What's more, he didn't have his family there to discuss things with. All he had to do was drive, and there were times, before he climbed into the car, when his nerves and his imagination got the better of him. He wanted, indeed needed, to prove to himself, to the team, and to his backers in New Zealand that they were right to have faith in him. But he was petrified he'd embarrass himself as he headed down to the pit garage in Silverstone for his first test session.

He barely managed two laps.

It was damp and I came around the corner on to the front straight; it was fast in those days, before they put in the chicane. I was on slicks and suddenly the thing turned hard right and I slammed it into the pit wall.

I was just warming things up and it caught me out.

I had never experienced anything like it. I was embarrassed, shocked, horrified and I thought they were going to put me on the next plane back to New Zealand.

As he slunk back to the pits fretting over how the mechanics had spent three days and nights getting the car ready for him and expecting to receive a right royal bollocking, he suddenly discovered the difference between a professional racing operation and the family firm back home.

'My whole career to that point had been about driving the car on the oil gauge and I suddenly found I'd stepped into a place where people said, "Oh well, these things happen, let's get on and get it fixed." It was kind of refreshing in that they were prepared to get me back out there, but I certainly didn't do myself any favours.'

The first race was at the same track and he went into it blind. He hadn't had time to learn the layout of the circuit because of the crash in testing, but, despite that, he got through practice and qualified for the race. Come race day he was suited up, sitting on the grid, waiting to start his first-ever motor race event in England. Sleet was swirling around his helmet. He'd never experienced anything like that, either.

Given the conditions, officials dithered over whether to start the race, eventually deciding that it could go ahead in the snow. It was a far cry from the soaring summer racing conditions of New Zealand and Australia. Nonetheless, Paul managed to finish in the top 10 and, this being Silverstone, there were other compensations. Since Silverstone was the home of the British Grand Prix, a number of Formula 1 teams were based there, and Murray Taylor suggested going for a walk to meet a few of the drivers. 'I said, "What? Can you do that?" and you could. We just rolled over the bridge and met a few of the drivers and I thought, wow! You could walk into the pits and talk to people. It was a small little community and it was definitely more casual then, but even so, I was amazed.'

His learning curve was increasing daily. The next race in the series was on one of the fastest circuits in the United Kingdom, Thruxton, just under a couple of hours' drive from London. It is open and flowing, and at least at this circuit Paul had a chance to do some testing before the race.

If Silverstone had delivered the worst-case scenario in the test session, then Thruxton was about to make up for it. So far as the British media was concerned, Paul Radisich was fresh off the plane from New Zealand (all paddocks and sheep), he had done a couple of seasons in Australia (all drought and flies), and he'd crashed in his first test session in England. Yet this unknown Antipodean went out and took pole position.

Of course, in an ideal world he would have gone on to win the race, but he didn't. It has to be remembered the racing format was quite different to what he'd been used to at home: for the first time in his life, he had to qualify and compete on the same day.

'Normally, overnight, you go through what you're going to do on the start line, but I didn't have that at Thruxton, and it was my first race there, so I wasn't quite mentally geared up to handle the start scenario.'

He had a coming together with another competitor and, although he was only sixth, he made an impression on the eventual winner of the championship, Johnny Dumfries:

> *Paul's arrival on the British F3 scene did cause something of a stir, because he was quick straight out of the box and no-one had ever heard of him before! I think it is fair to say that he made his mark.*

Johnny Dumfries is, in fact, a Scottish peer: the 7th Marquess of Bute, Earl of Dumfries. The family home is Mount Stuart House on the Isle of Bute, but he has always preferred not to use his title. He went on from Formula 3 to race one season in Formula 1 with Team Lotus in 1986, with team-mate the legendary Ayrton Senna. In 1988, he was a member of the Silk Cut Jaguar team which won the Le Mans 24-Hour event.

Paul eventually finished seventh in the series, to exhibit what Murray Taylor calls enormous talent. The pole position at Thruxton had confirmed his talent, but he wasn't going anywhere else. He had reached a dead end.

Even though the team was littered with Kiwis speaking the same dialect, in the end business took precedence. Paul had been unable to compete in all of the Formula 3 events in the series because he simply didn't have enough money. The lottery back home that had sounded such a good idea in principle didn't hold out in reality. The policing of it was suspect, and no one had a clear idea of how many tickets had been sold. In the end this left Paul underfunded and underdone. He didn't have a proverbial bean to his name. He headed home to recuperate financially and emotionally, not realizing that he'd have to sit on the sidelines for another two seasons as far as his England ambitions were concerned.

The wait would not be entirely fallow, however, as he went back to work for his father. But unlike the first time, he wasn't working as a grease monkey. This time he was put in charge of selling blended oil for a company that Frank had started. 'It was a financial necessity for the family and for me, because we were all financially exhausted,' recalls Paul. 'I was in charge of the Auckland area, and the job gave me the opportunity to hone my selling skills. At the same time, I was on the lookout for someone who could help me get back into motor racing. That wasn't going to happen without the right sort of backing.'

Like most good things, it didn't happen overnight, but it did happen. About a year after he came home, Paul had made the acquaintance of a young film producer, an avid petrol-head and part-time racer by the name of Rob Whitehouse. His film credits at the time included *Battletruck* and *Scarecrow*. They first met when Rob was thinking of buying a March from Frank (which didn't happen), and a few years later they met again when Paul was beginning his first full season in Formula Atlantic in New Zealand.

There was something about Paul, something special in the way he conducted himself on and off the track. You could see he had talent and he was a nice guy as well.

By the time Paul had returned from England, Rob Whitehouse and his friend Andrew Bagnall (a former owner of Gulliver's Travel, a successful driver in his own right, and long a supporter of New Zealand motor racing) had formulated a plan to set up a Group A touring-car race-team. They decided they could 'wrap' Paul into the funding arrangements.

These two businessmen were established entrepreneurs, and there is no question their modus operandi for Paul was a first for New Zealand motor racing. It was certainly ambitious, but in the context of the times not overly so. In effect, Rob would treat Paul like a racehorse. He would give him enough oats to keep him happy, pat him on the nose, dig him in the ribs, slap his flank, and send him out to race.

A consortium of investors, banking on Paul's pedigree, was to provide the funding. It was no more, nor any less, risky than investing in a filly or a gelding or, for that matter, bank-rolling a fledgling film, which was where the idea had originated. Paul certainly wasn't a filly, and as time revealed he hadn't been gelded. But he was certainly a star with potential.

Rob Whitehouse and Andrew Bagnall purchased the championship-winning Merkur Sierra from Andy Rouse in the UK and put David Oxton in the car for the Group A championship. They also bought a Group A Escort for the long-distance events; Paul ended up being the first to drive it, because Rob, who was supposed to have the wheel for the Bay Park event, only arrived back from the UK a day or two before the race and was just too jet-lagged to compete. Paul got pole. He didn't finish the race, but the Escort was only a theatrical aside to the main play.

The target was to send Paul to England for another crack at Formula 3 for the 1986 season, once again with Murray Taylor's team. This time his team-mate would be Damon Hill, and if ever there was a son of motoring's aristocracy, he was it. Damon's father, Graham, had won the Formula 1 World Championship twice (in 1962 and 1968), but had died in a light aircraft crash in 1975, along with several other members of his Embassy Team. His son, beginning his own journey towards Formula 1, was the emotional favourite of every British racing fan and more than a few sponsors. In the Formula 3 team, he already had what Rob Whitehouse calls a 'coterie of trendy people around him, the groovy set'.

That might have been so at the race track. At home in London, Damon and Georgie Hill had a small flat that was so basic that they had to feed coins into a meter to get the electricity to work and to heat the water. In many ways, the Hills were no different to Paul Radisich and his girlfriend, Louise Pedersen, who had come to England and was working for a secretarial agency as a temp. Both women were keeping their men alive, feeding them, clothing them and paying the rent, all in the interests of motor racing.

Paul and Louise flatted in an attached townhouse with 'ghastly carpet and curtains', which they shared with an American who was racing Formula Ford 2000. They needed him to help with the rent, and, as a part-time sideline and for the same reason, Paul became a driver training instructor at the Silverstone Racing School. Louise went to as many events as she could, but it wasn't always possible because she was the breadwinner and had to work even if, as she says, Paul relied heavily on someone being there for support:

> *There was all the washing and ironing and cooking, and he always liked you being at official functions and so on, to write his reports, send faxes, send race results off. And he relied on you getting things to the racetrack besides his own helmet and race suit.*

They were serious racers on the track, but it didn't stop them larking about off it. In Zandvoort in Holland, Damon Hill, Perry McCarthy and few of the others had gone out to dinner together.

They tucked in, enjoyed themselves and then decided to do a runner from the restaurant. Paul didn't want to be landed with the bill (and he didn't have any money anyway), so he left too and headed back to where they were all staying, which was in a kind of motel with dormitory-like accommodation. They had all been asleep for about an hour when the police turned up: 'We all kept silent or pleaded ignorance, which wasn't hard because none of us could speak Dutch and the police eventually left without making any arrests.'

There were times during their stay in England when Paul and Louise were so short of money that they were handed around hospitable friends of friends for the weekend, a bit like pass-the-parcel paupers. As a result, they got to know some of the people surrounding Damon Hill quite well. They became acquainted with Jack and Joy Bridge (friends of Damon's mother), and would stay in a little flat attached to their house in Surrey.

Murray Taylor was locked into a deal with Ron Tauranac to use Ralts, but they were uncompetitive against the new Reynards. Damon Hill was generally faster than Paul, not because he was the superior driver but, as Murray concedes, because his Ralt had been fitted with the better components, with the leftovers going to Paul. At the time Rob Whitehouse thought Paul had essentially been hung out to dry in the team, but admits he wasn't always available to back him up.

Paul was on his own, there was no immediate family support, and he was thrown in the deep end. I went to the UK when I could, but I didn't have much time available because I had some troubles of my own at the time. I would have liked to have been Paul's manager, but I took my eye off the ball because I was in New Zealand.

Paul had returned to Taylor's team for the honourable reason that he and his backers owed Murray money. They were told that since there were debts still outstanding, no other team would take him on. Murray was operating under financial pressures, too; and at one point he was so persistent in the way he was pestering Frank Radisich to pay up that Frank disconnected the telephone. The season that had started with promise soon slithered south. The best Paul could manage was a podium finish with a third at Snetterton: 'It was the wrong car that season and it just didn't gel at all. Murray did his best, but he was under all sorts of financial constraints as well.'

For Murray Taylor it was the worst year he'd had in the category. The following year he packed up the family and came home. He was still working with professional sport, but this time in yachting with Peter Blake and the Steinlager round-the-world campaign. Murray enjoyed working with Paul Radisich, who was fast (given the right equipment) and thoroughly professional in his attitude.

In hindsight, Paul realizes he might have done things differently in England, but it is easy to be wise years after the event. He is pleased he gave it a go, but says the fact that the timing and the opportunities by-passed him are just the way it is. The politics of motor racing are manifold, and Rob Whitehouse believes that if they had been more aggressive in their approach and had realized they could have jumped into another team, they would have done so. But in the end it was all about money they didn't quite have.

Nonetheless, Paul always felt he was capable, and he decided to prove it to himself. He organized a Formula 3 test in order, he says, to discover whether he was kidding himself. The Madgwick team he tested with had won the championship with Andy Wallace. 'I pretty much had my bags packed to leave the UK and, for what consolation it was worth, I needed to try and prove I could drive a car: I just needed to be in the right one.'

The Reynard F3 car they were using was the first to use a carbon-fibre chassis; it was the 'in' car to have. Within half a dozen laps Paul had equalled Andy Wallace's time, and within another half-dozen laps he had improved on that again by around 0.2 of a second. It was the quickest any driver of any Reynard F3 car had ever been around Snetterton at that point.

Madgwick wanted him for the following season and came up with an offer. They were even able to supplement his budget to help things along. But such are the sums of money involved that it still wasn't enough.

I knew I'd have to find £100,000 to do the season, and there was no way it would happen. By the end of '86, I'd lost my motivation. I needed money and power, and couldn't get either. When I look back, I'm disappointed I didn't use the time more wisely when I was in the UK.

Formula 1 was the goal I had set, and so many

top drivers in that had stepped out of the Formula 3 series — it was where everyone went. If I'd gone back to Formula 3 and dominated the way I had in '84, I think it would have been a different story for me.

Maybe I didn't put enough emphasis on trying to make it, but as a one-man-band trying to get into Formula 1 I always knew the odds were really stacked against me.

Chapter 5

You do know where we come from, don't you?

To have another chance to run in front of those guys was quite exciting, but it never got me anywhere. You needed someone in front of you, pushing the wheelbarrow out in front and saying to watch this kid race, but at the end of the day it's just a noise going round and round the track and they are in their own little capsule.

By the end of 1987, Paul had two seasons in Formula 3 under his belt, with some good results and some less-impressive results; the latter not necessarily due to any lack of talent. If he was to make progress in the formula, Paul needed a group or an organization behind him, but that didn't materialize. He was essentially on his own.

Rather than come scurrying home with his tail between his legs, Paul granted himself a holiday in the USA. He had kept in contact with friends and acquaintances while he was in Britain, and one of those was Dave White, who was running in the Supervee Series with Garvin Brown Racing in the USA. Dave invited him over for a holiday and, although Paul didn't know it then, that innocent invitation would lead to other opportunities which would take him literally on to different tracks.

Paul Radisich was about to impress Americans, even if they couldn't pronounce his name and didn't know where in the world New Zealand might be.

One of the many people he had met while racing Formula 3 in Britain was American driver Dave Simpson. His father, Bill, owned Simpson Racewear, so Paul went to visit the showroom in Los Angeles and found a big, fat American standing behind the counter.

'Are you Radish?' he bellowed. 'I've seen you in Formula 3.'

Paul was in the right place at the right time. Bill Simpson wanted him to drive his car at Tampa, Florida, in a round of the Supervee Championship. The permanent driver, Jeff Simpson (another of Bill's sons), was suffering sinus problems and couldn't compete. The next thing Paul knew, he was being fitted for a race suit at the back of a workshop that was crawling with the Mexicans manufacturing them, and the following day he was on his way to the other side of the country.

He was quickest in practice . . . before the engine blew — exploded like a bomb, he says — which meant he had to start from the back of the grid. However, he worked his way up the field to finish in the top four, and Bill invited him to the next round at St Petersburg, also in Florida. There he got pole, and with it the chance to change the face of the Supervee Championship.

'Didier Theys was expected to be crowned champion and I could have got in the way of that because I had pole. I remembered I had to get second, but I was right up his gearbox and I could have passed him, but I didn't want to be the guy who screwed up his championship.'

Bill Simpson invited him back for the following season, and Paul, naturally, expected to do the entire season. It didn't turn out that way, and the big man's inconsistency became a worry.

One minute I was the son, and the next minute he'd throw me out of the car and say I was fired — I was an arsehole and a burden to him and I had to get out of the shop.

I'd say, 'You're joking!', but no he wasn't, and we'd miss a couple of rounds and have to rely on people's generosity to survive. I needed to race to get prize money.

Then he'd come back and tell me I was in the next race.

The cause of the problem was Scott Acheson, who was considered something of the golden boy, the next American protégé; and were it not for Paul Radisich beating him, he might have been. The situation became delicately political, and Bill eventually said to Paul that it would be best if he were not involved.

'I was living on 10 per cent of the prize money, which was OK because it kept me going, but to get a start and then to get chopped off was a pain in the neck.'

Fortunately, Louise Pedersen was there to support him. She had left her New Zealand job at Lifeworks Clothing and headed to America, too. They would stay in the cheapest hotels possible, and on more than one occasion slept in the car to save money. It was a $450 Fiat with different-coloured doors — blue, white and rust. They were constantly feeding it water, and Paul would tune it every other day or so. The couple never knew where the next dollop of money would come from, so Robyn and Frank frequently paid their credit-card bill.

Paul was a temp for hire, which meant he had to turn up to a race meeting just to see if there might be some takers. A glimmer of a more permanent opportunity appeared in Cleveland, when he was approached by a little man whom Paul thought might have originally hailed from somewhere in the Middle East. Kerry Agapiou told him that his regular driver wasn't able to make the grid, so Paul jumped in the car and got sixth. He was offered the chance to drive for the rest of the season, but had to turn it down because he was committed to Simpson, however flaky that arrangement might be. He was also driving a big Trans-Am for Bruce Jenner on any occasion he could manage. Anything else would have been far, far too much, even if he did have to earn a crust.

Despite the uncertainty of it all, America gave Paul considerable momentum to start another New Zealand season, and he flew back home feeling more buoyed than he had for a couple of years. It was the first time he had raced a single-seater in his own country for five years — since 1983, in fact, when he had come second in the national championship and won the Bruce McLaren Young Driver of the Year Award. Now he returned as the one to watch, as a potential winner of New Zealand's most coveted trophy: the New Zealand International Grand Prix.

The Ralt RT4 he was using for the New Zealand Global Series sported an iridescent colour scheme for 1988: an eye-blinding orangey-pink of the sort that had first appeared on men's socks in the 'sixties. If nothing else, it looked great on television. It would look even better if he could win the event. He did.

That year, everything we attempted seemed to work. I had done a lot of racing up to that point; we had sponsorship organized; we had brand new components for the car; we had done a reasonable amount of testing; and we were fully organized.

In the race itself, Kenny Smith chased me all the way; he was on top of his game, going hard out, and I had to watch the mirror constantly. I knew if I made one little slip-up, I would be gone. He was driving the wheels off his car and was on my tail all the way — it was a real nuisance, actually — and I knew he'd be there to pick up the pieces if I made a mistake.

He didn't, and at long last the Paul Radisich name was able to be written into the record books and onto the handsome New Zealand Motor Cup, which is today valued at around NZ$100,000. It's inscribed with some of the top motor-racing names in the world: Stirling Moss, Jack Brabham, John Surtees, Bruce McLaren, Graham Hill, Chris Amon — rarefied company, indeed.

I remember as I crossed the line I just felt huge relief, because this was the race to win. It was a big event, which Frank had tried to win years before. He'd built the engine, and that's a massive part of the preparation, so it allowed the family to win, too.

As chief mechanic for Paul's various racing cars, Frank occasionally had to swallow comments about his engineering abilities from behind the pit wall by those who thought they knew better. This win, then, was a sweet response.

Paul got out of the car and gave Kenny Smith a hug, both of them appreciating the effort and the trust between them on the track. He walked over to Frank and hugged him, too. Frank was in tears.

Shortly afterwards, Paul shot over to Australia for a one-off drive with Graham Watson's team for the Formula 2 Australian Grand Prix, and won that race by nearly a lap. Once again he was driving in an under-card race to a Formula 1 event — and sometimes these things pay off. Shortly afterwards, Paul received an invitation to contest the Supervee Series back in America with a new team, and for the first time in a long while he had a concrete proposal to contest an entire season.

The man doing the asking was Dave Conti, who had started at the bottom of the racing ladder sweeping the floor at Ralt America, and in just three years had left there to run his own team. His workshop was next-door to a chicken coop in Indianapolis. Dave McMillan's team occupied the other side, and the Kiwis who worked there, including Louise Pedersen's father, Garry, were so astonished at Dave Conti's rapid progress in the sport they called him 'the rocket scientist'. Dave Conti called them the 'evil' Ralt America, and Paul's arrival created a small problem for Garry: 'If Paul came around home we weren't supposed to talk to him about what we were doing, because he was driving for the opposition and here he was, carting out my daughter.'

Frequently, the Kiwi mechanics were operating on as much of a shoestring as some of the drivers. The wealthier teams in the series were probably blissfully unaware that there were Kiwis on a foraging mission in the dead of night, sticking their beaks into waste bins pecking for parts that the Americans had thrown out.

Dave Conti had a sponsorship deal for US$50,000 to run three cars in 10 races, so it, too, was a lean operation, with just five people working on the three cars. The first race was in Dallas, Texas, and in qualifying Paul was about four seconds faster in the wet than anyone else. He eventually finished second in the race because of a slipping clutch.

The next race in the schedule was held on the streets of Detroit, Motor City, Motown, on a quirky circuit of tight 90-degree turns and short straight sections. Paul's race was on the same card as a Formula 1 event, officially titled the United States Grand Prix East, and Frank and Robyn flew in especially.

Paul qualified on pole, and come race day he led from green flag to chequered flag. Frank is adamant the win justified his decision to start his son off in motocross, because in his view Paul's ability to rapidly read a circuit had made its presence felt.

Just before the race, the circuit announcer went back through the history of the event, and apparently no one had got pole unless they had been there three, four or

maybe five times, because in Detroit you couldn't even
walk around the circuit beforehand.

When it came to the race, we thought when the flag
dropped the other cars behind him would swamp him
and that would be it, but when he got the green he just
took off and absolutely cleared out.

The next day, a Monday morning, *USA Today* was published with a full race report. On one side of the page was a photo and story of the Brazilian superstar Ayrton Senna, who had won the Formula 1 event in the McLaren Honda. Given equal billing on the other side of the page was Paul Radisich, an improbable and mysterious winner of the supporting Supervee event from a country most readers didn't know existed, and many of those who did know of it probably couldn't locate it on a map. Ayrton Senna, on the other hand, knew exactly where Paul was from and what he had done. They met at the press conference.

Senna came up to me and said congratulations, and
said he had watched some of the races and that I'd
blown them away.

He asked about the track and whether it had changed
from the day before, and asked for my thoughts, so in
that sense I guess I gave Senna some advice. He shook
my hand, went away and won the race.

Paul went on to win again at Niagara Falls and Cleveland, and the little Kiwi from New Zealand in the black car began to be seriously noticed. Americans who had never heard of Paul Radisich or New Zealand before were suddenly hearing a whole lot about one and rushing for an atlas to find out about the other. Other drivers would lay bets — not on who would get first, because that was the little critter from Noo Zealand — but on who would get second. Dave Conti says Paul was teaching them a thing or two on the track in the process.

I remember another competitor asking Paul where he braked for the chicane before the pit straight at Detroit. Paul looked at him in a funny way and said he didn't brake at all, that he was flat through that section. The look on the guy's face as he walked away mumbling was priceless!

All in all, Paul had five wins in the series, but the golden run didn't last. Dave Conti went to New Jersey imagining what he could do with the $10,500 prize money that had been put up for the race. Unfortunately, he didn't get it. Paul spun on some oil, deposited courtesy of a back marker with a blown engine. His car slammed into the barriers, so Dave Conti had to buy a new tub and fix everything else. Paul desperately wanted to win the last race at St Petersburg in Florida, but the same old story surfaced: the money ran out, and Conti had to tell him that he couldn't afford to go through the winter if Paul ran into someone else's bad luck. Paul had no choice but to return to New Zealand. Before that, though, he zipped across the Atlantic to try to get a drive with Vern Schuppan's Porsche team in the world sports-car championship. He missed out to Czechoslovakian Tomas Mezera, who now judges the driving standards in V8 Supercars.

At this stage in his career, saloon cars were some way from Paul's mind. It had been eight years since he'd raced the little Toyota Trueno in New Zealand, and he hadn't raced what could be called a road car since then, but an invitation to compete on one of the world's iconic race tracks isn't to be ignored. Bathurst, BMW and a man called Bill beckoned.

The BMW was an M3 version and was owned by New Zealander Bill Bryce. For his introduction to the Mt Panorama circuit, Paul was paired with the young German driver Ludwig Finauer. The car was too small to be an outright winner against the might of the Ford Sierra Cosworths, but it was a fun opportunity for a drive. When he got there, he couldn't see what all the fuss was about.

I would see Peter Brock and Dick Johnson running around and know that they had all the sponsorship and were doing really well, and I would look at them sideways and, being a purist, I didn't see why that should be. I didn't appreciate what it was all about because I guess at that time I was narrow-minded.

I considered single-seaters to be proper cars and when you hop out of a single-seater and into a saloon car, it's like driving a bowl of jelly. I viewed touring cars as something I wouldn't get satisfaction out of,

*because you can only drive to the limits of the car, not
yourself.*

Paul decided to remain in New Zealand to contest the Global
Series again the following year, 1989, and to have another shot
at winning the domestic Grand Prix in the Swift. It was, and
always will be, a rare feat to win any Grand Prix back-to-back,
and against the odds that's exactly what he did. He led from start
to finish, and when he came into the pits he was elated.

That's when officials told him he had jumped the start and he
was given a time penalty. It pushed him well down the official
finishing order. He hadn't been given any warning during the
race. Those were the days before in-car radios, but, even so, if
he'd been black-flagged and had to come into the pits for a drive-
through, at least he would have known and could possibly have
fought his way back up to the front.

The team protested the decision, and the whole thing went
to an official hearing at New Zealand Motorsport headquarters
in Wellington. Paul took along his long-time family friend and
car dealer, Nick Begovic, who had served some time as a motor-
sport official and was used to the committee structure of the
governing body and aware of the sometimes incomprehensible
decision-making of the sport. American Dean Hall and the man
running him in the Global Series, Graeme Lawrence, all travelled
south together. 'Big Nick had his day in the sun and did it well,
but at the end of the day the ruling stood. We had to cop it on
the chin, and we all felt we had been hard done by.'

The year was significant for Paul Radisich for another reason.

He was invited to drive in the Nissan Mobil Series in New Zealand with none other than the king among Australian racing princes, Peter Brock, in a BMW M3. The catalyst for securing the drive was Brock's team manager, Alan Gow, who had helped Paul out as a sponsor when he drove the little Formula 3 single-seater in Australia for Graham Watson and who had been impressed by him.

It wasn't a shot in the dark to pair him up with Peter Brock, because Paul had driven an M3 the year before; he knew the car and he knew the track.

After battling the makeshift and gruelling harbour-side circuit in downtown Wellington for the first round of the series, they headed to the Pukekohe track the following weekend, where they clinched the series. In the process, they defeated some of the more fancied names from world touring cars, people like Roberto Ravaglia, Emmanuele Pirro, Steve Soper and Aussies Dick Johnson and Larry Perkins. Of course, Paul didn't know it then, but he was going to meet some of those drivers again in a couple of other countries in two other major series.

Although some people would consider driving saloon cars a fallback position for a driver who can't secure a single-seater drive, Paul found that he was in the company of highly talented racers, and there were some definite advantages to the class. It kept him race-fit, whether he had a roof over his head or not, and indeed, his single-seater experience was considered to be something of a bonus in a saloon car. However, he still didn't consider saloon cars to be his destiny.

Paul had been running the single-seater Swift throughout 1989, but had relinquished that in favour of a Reynard for 1990 after he and Graham Lorimer struck a deal with Adrian Reynard and Rick Gorn that allowed them to use one of their new chassis in New Zealand.

We told them we could improve the sales of their Formula Atlantic cars and said they couldn't miss this opportunity because New Zealand was such a great market and so on. To our surprise they gave us a car, all the spares and development parts! It doesn't get much better than that.

They had acquired the car that Jeff Andretti had been using in America without much success. They called on the technical manager of Toyota New Zealand, Ross Morten, and with his help they were able to put in a Toyota engine. They promptly won the first race at Bay Park. It was the first time that Reynard had ever won a race in the first year of Formula Atlantic production, and Reynard went on to sell a lot of cars off the back of that success.

It was also through Graham Lorimer that he organized another formula car test in England, and once again it was with Madgwick Motorsport. Graham was working for the team at the time, and the car of choice for Paul was a Formula 3000.

The category had been created in 1985 to replace Formula 2 as a quicker but more affordable option, and it was specifically viewed by the FIA as a direct stepping-stone to Formula 1. Compared with the Formula 3 car Paul had driven in Murray Taylor's team, it was a move up in terms of speed and handling ability. So Paul turned up to Snetterton.

> *I slotted into the car and was going quite well for a while. I came out of the bomb hole and had probably done a few too many laps and got the left wheel caught on the edge of the track, and because these cars run so low to the ground it just sort of skidded and went off into the tyre wall.*
>
> *I had punted it off the track and pretty much straight away I reckoned I had done my dash and I wasn't going to be doing any more testing for them.*

When he came back into the pits, there wasn't much talking going on. He wasn't asked back.

Over in Australia, however, the legendary touring car king Dick Johnson had been watching Paul's progress and invited him to drive a Sierra Cosworth with Englishman Jeff Allam at Bathurst in 1991. They came close to winning, but in the end had to settle for second place. Back in New Zealand again, Paul teamed up with Australian driver Michael Preston to win the Nissan Mobil Series for a second time before another season of single-seaters beckoned.

Paul continued with the Reynard in New Zealand for another season, and not long after the New Zealand series had ended he received a telephone call from Ted Titmus in California, inviting him to contest the Long Beach Grand Prix. A workshop and all sponsorships were arranged, he said, so Paul packed up the Reynard and some spares and flew everything to the West Coast. Perhaps if he had known in advance what was about to happen he might have called the Titmus deal 'Titsup' and called the whole thing off. On the Friday before the race, he and his mechanic, Les Laidlaw, found their way to the workshop, only to find it locked. 'I phoned Ted to ask what was happening, and he said I owed him money! I asked him what for and he didn't say, but he said the car had been impounded and it was his car!'

Legally, Reynard owned the chassis, Paul owned the pit equipment and all the running paraphernalia, and Toyota New Zealand owned the engines — but there was Titmus making claim to the lot. Paul called the Los Angeles Police Department, but they weren't particularly interested. Eventually, and after much haggling, Titmus released the car, but with it came a bodyguard — a very large, very black bodyguard — to stand over the car and Paul.

It was bizarre. Ted thought I was going to run off with the car. The arrangement was that I could race the car, but if I damaged anything I had to replace it. I think I bent a front wing. There I was in the race with all sorts of financial dramas swirling around my head. I didn't have any spares, and even had to borrow a wheel from someone.

I got second and Ted eventually bought the car from Reynard, but I think there was a lot more going on behind the scenes than I knew about.

Paul came home without the Reynard, and up popped saloon cars once more. He went back to Bathurst, this time partnering Terry Shiel in the second of the Dick Johnson Racing Ford Sierra RS500s, but they failed to finish. It almost didn't matter, because Paul was still being recognized and he was asked to race in Japan for Team Stellar.

The Japanese team owner had three cars to choose from: Formula 3, Formula 3000 (known as Formula Nippon) and a BMW M3 touring car. Paul was expected to arrive at the Fuji circuit fresh off the plane and, although he'd never seen the circuit before, then jump in the F3000 and break the lap record first time out. 'You drive, you drive' is how the owner phrased it, flapping his arms towards the single-seater.

This owner also thought that Paul should shed some weight — a somewhat bemusing request given that Paul was (and still is) slightly built — but to keep him happy, Paul said he'd try. In the end, however, the owner didn't consider him good enough for the single-seater Formula Nippon, because his times weren't instantly up to scratch. Nonetheless, Paul was offered the opportunity to pair with Irishman Derek Higgins in a BMW M3 for the Fuji 500 event. If Paul didn't know the circuit, he certainly knew the car. The other regular formula drivers, Roland Ratzenberger and Andrew Gilbert-Scott, formed part of the two-car team for the long-distance event. Paul and Derek Higgins won their class.

Since this was his first trip to Japan, Paul had decided to do some sightseeing and his uncle, Tony Radisich, had arranged for a tour guide especially. On the Sunday morning of the event, he was to meet the guide at the main gate of the race track with some passes. There were 100,000 people there that day, and to Paul they all looked alike: 'I duly positioned myself at the gate, but I couldn't tell who was a tour guide and who wasn't, so I didn't go sightseeing!'

If hopping between open-wheel and tin-top racing cars wasn't enough to keep him going, Paul was talked into driving in the New Zealand Truck Racing Series in a green Kenworth truck everyone called Kermit. Denny Hulme was in the Eta Ripples Scania, so Paul figured if it was good enough for 'The Bear', it was good enough for him.

At Pukekohe, the throttle jammed open on Paul's truck and it 'fell' on its side at the top of the hill. He never went near the thing again. Robyn Radisich was in a Mitsubishi at the same event, but Paul was so sceptical of the big behemoths ever producing anything but grief that he pressured her to walk away as well, while she still could.

Three months later, he and Peter Brock won the Nissan Mobil Series. For Paul it was the third time he'd done so.

In the midst of this fairly busy driving year, discussions were continuing over Paul's future in America, or anywhere else for that matter, because the burning ambition to get back on the track in a single-seater had not yet diminished. Even at this stage, Paul thought that somehow, some way, Formula 1 might still be worth aiming for. It would be a long shot, but if the best team, a good car and competent personnel could be bought with the right money in Formula 3 or Formula 3000, would it be worth pursuing the ultimate dream?

He wanted to give himself every opportunity to prove his worth.

Chapter 6

Nightmares, dreams and guardian angels

To have my own racing car, my own road car, my own flat to stay in, being able to focus on the one thing, to have a goal, was something I'd never really had before and it was pretty special.

B y 1992, Paul Radisich found himself in a professional cul de sac. His ambition was intact, but it always seemed to be hard up against reality, meaning money. There was always more than enough of one, but never quite enough of the other. One of New Zealand's motor-racing stars was skint.

Other New Zealanders had also trod the single-seater path that Paul and his family had actively chosen, but none of them had had to bring thousands of pounds to a team to purchase a drive. By the mid-eighties, when Paul was eyeing Europe, money was doing the talking and many a fledgling champion from this part of the world was gazumped by the bank balances available to kids from South America and Europe, whose family millions were being invested in their futures. It was very hard indeed to compete off-the-track like that, particularly from New Zealand, where the 'Pacific peso' exchange rate was a major impediment.

Paul had enjoyed some spectacular results in open-wheel racing, but without the cash it wasn't enough to secure him employment as a full-time driver. There were also some 'other' results; in other words, instances where he was nowhere near the front end, for whatever reason — a state of affairs that actor and comedian Stephen Fry calls 'differently first'.

Still undaunted, Paul was rushing to prepare the Formula Pacific single-seater for the New Zealand summer series and trying to put a deal together to race Indy Lights in the States. It had been nearly eight years since he'd first landed in England and raced Formula 3; and around five years since he had headed to America and made a bit of a name for himself. In the last three of those years he had slowly eased himself into saloon cars with a number of drives in New Zealand and Australia in a variety of long-distance events, so if he was ever going to change to saloons and if the financial rewards were enticing, it might be worth considering. He might not have been actively seeking a saloon-car drive, but he was still aware of the possibilities in that class, and in fact he'd been watching others shine while driving saloon cars.

I remember seeing Roberto Ravaglia in Wellington using all of the track, and it's quite ironic, because I remember thinking in those days that I could be a touring-car driver with my name on the side of the car. I would look at Jeff Allam and Steve Soper and the other works drivers and it took my fancy I guess.

That line of thought started formulating from about

1990, and it drove me to go back to the UK and to keep
talking to all the teams that were running up there.

Paul had been knocking on doors for years, pleading with companies for sponsorship, tearing around the country, around the world, battling away on his own. He was a one-man-band, although he did have valuable help from the various people surrounding him: his family, his girlfriends, his mates. Remarkably, he had managed to keep going for over a decade. Yet he hadn't had a decent wage in his life at that point, and some of those he was competing against in single-seaters were by then a dozen years his junior.

There was nothing permanent about his life at all and he barely had two beans to rub together, yet he was held up as a yardstick by those who wanted to follow him to Europe or the US. Most people in New Zealand looking at this peripatetic life imagined he was on the pig's back. At some point, though, the mentors, the sponsors and the driver would have to collectively call a halt to pursuing the dream.

Paul wasn't consciously considering an alternative: he was focused on competing in the New Zealand single-seater series. Until, that is, he took a call from Australian Alan Gow, who invited him to join Andy Rouse's Ford Mondeo programme to contest the British Touring Car Championship. That telephone call backed him into a corner. It was crunch time.

In my entire career I never had completed a full
overseas series. There had been years of jumping from

seat to seat, from team to team, from place to place. Even when I'd get the budget together, I'd be up against people who had both the budget and the experience of racing every weekend.

Alan Gow was working for Andy Rouse, selling special-built, road-going Ford Sierra Sapphire Cosworths based on the touring-car racing version. But he had another role: he was helping to run the British Touring Car Championship. Andy Rouse needed another driver in the team, and Alan recommended Paul. Amazing as it now seems, when Paul got that telephone call, he hesitated. He didn't leap in the air with elation at the offer. He dithered — and Alan couldn't believe it.

Paul's very good behind the wheel, but he's the most indecisive person I've met. I phoned him anyway, said I might be able to get him a works drive in the BTCC.

He said he had the opportunity to do Indy Lights in the States.

Here he was, scrounging around trying to get the money, never getting a full deal . . . I was incredulous and said, 'Are you f***ing kidding me? You're getting the opportunity to get a paid Ford works drive and you're weighing it up between that and scratching around in the States trying to make it!'

Paul still believed that he was on the verge of being able to do well in America. He knew he could drive, he knew he could win in single-seaters, he just needed the right amount of money. He'd been working hard on a deal to race in Indy Lights, but suddenly, with the offer of a paid drive in one of the best teams in British Touring Cars, the effort would have to be shelved. It would mean retiring from single-seaters.

He hesitated, for at least an hour. He knew it wasn't Formula 1, but he also knew it was a dream drive. He phoned Alan Gow back and accepted the offer.

There were other connections that got Paul to Andy Rouse Racing in England. First, the great Peter Brock had driven with Paul and rated his abilities highly. Secondly, Andy Rouse had driven at Bathurst with Brocky in 1989, and it was there that he had met Paul, who at the time was contesting Bathurst in partnership with Brad Jones. Andy Rouse had thereafter followed Paul's career with more interest, so the Kiwi was in the view-finder of at least two people who would have an important influence on his future. But other, probably even more significant decision-makers had serious doubts about him.

Ford Motor Company in the UK had appointed Andy Rouse to run and manage their BTCC contract, and the boffins, the so-called motor-sport experts within Ford, were initially sceptical about his choice of Paul as a driver. Because they knew nothing about this man who came from the other side of the world, they considered his selection to be something of a gamble. Andy, however, persuaded them to think otherwise, and not just because of Paul's driving abilities: 'Paul was reasonably cheap at that stage! But we chose the drivers because we were in charge of the team. We knew he was hungry, and it was a great opportunity for him.'

What was 'reasonably cheap' to Andy Rouse was a considerable amount of money to Paul Radisich. Ostensibly, he was paid £50,000, but when Alan Gow negotiated the deal, the canny operator included in the small print that Paul had to pay him a whopping 50 per cent of total annual income. Paul ended up driving for Andy Rouse in the first year of British Touring Cars for a wage less than a competent secretary could expect to receive. Compared with nearly all the other drivers in the British Touring Car Championship, he was practically on Skid Row.

On the positive side, for the first time in his life Paul didn't have to scout around for opportunities that might or might not crop up, or look for money that might or might not materialize to keep his body, soul and ambition intact. He no longer had to rely on his girlfriend to feed, clothe and house him. He could live reasonably well. He was a fully paid professional racing driver with security of tenure for an entire season.

It also meant, of course, that Radisich Inc., the family firm, had to take a step back. For the first time in their lives, they were not heavily involved. Frank says they accepted it; they knew the score and understood the full implications of their son becoming a professional driver.

Paul spent the Christmas of 1992 at home with the family, but by the time the 1993 New Zealand summer series was in full swing and the local drivers were busy thrashing around the track in their open-wheelers, he was facing a winter in England at a small flat he rented in Leamington Spa. According to him, his job was the result of 'Andy Rouse hiring a dumb little Kiwi', but clearly a number of people thought he was the man for the job. Paul had helped to ensure that he got the job by telephoning Andy Rouse on a number of occasions, keeping his profile high.

He had also pestered the crack German Schnitzer team, but those pleas went unheeded. At the time, they took the attitude that, unless the driver was a European, he wouldn't get a look in, end of story. In 1993, they were running BMWs with British driver Steve Soper and his new team-mate, the rookie German Joachim 'Smokin' Jo' Winkelhock. Having been turned down by Schnitzer, Paul suddenly found he had a chance to drive against them in another highly regarded team. In February, he turned up at Rouse Engineering for his first look at the team and the workshop.

It really didn't sink in until I arrived and saw these body shells lying around the floor with my name on the side. Before then, I'd only shared a car with others; it had always been Radisich and someone else, and suddenly, here was me! And here was a brand-new Cosworth!

For a guy who had come from a rusty Fiat in the USA where to stop the thing I needed to put my foot through the firewall, it was sensational, but Andy had filled Ford up with all the right juices to convince them that I was worth having.

Andy and Alan had been pushing the barrow to make it all work, and Alan made sure of it by suggesting, not too subtly, that Paul wouldn't let him down. He wanted to protect his £25,000 investment, after all. However, there was one more factor that had contributed to Paul's appointment: the name of the car.

Mondeo is derived from the Latin *mundus*, meaning 'world' and was the first product of Ford's global initiative. It was to replace the successful Sierra, and the design and build was shared between the USA and Europe. It would be sold under the Mondeo name around the world, so having a Kiwi in the driver's seat wasn't going to add confusion to the company's marketing plans. A world car could, in a marketing sense, cope with a driver from anywhere in the world.

It is important to put the calibre of the team that Paul was joining into perspective.

Andy Rouse is the most successful driver in the history of British Touring Cars, even taking into account today's increased number of races in the schedule. Significantly, he brought an engineering background to the sport. He had self-built a couple of cars in his teens, then moved to Formula Ford. He went on to work for Broadspeed, the race engineering company set up by Ralph Broad, and switched to saloon-car racing in 1972 in the Ford Escort Mexico Series. In 1981, he set up his own engineering company (taking many former Broadspeed employees with him when that company went into liquidation), and Ford gave him the works contract to build and drive the Sierra Cosworths. It was a highly successful relationship. He acquired the Mondeo contract for the 1993 British Touring Car season, and at that point hired Paul Radisich.

Paul's appointment also coincided with the healthy public positioning of British Touring Cars. By the time he arrived on the scene, there were 17 races, held over 14 weeks. Some of the world's top touring-car drivers from seven different countries, racing eight different manufacturers' models, were involved in an often furious and definitely highly egotistical competition that produced a thoroughly entertaining championship. It was the classic Europe versus England versus Japan shooting match and made great television.

Since one of our own was competing amongst this lot, driving against some of the top Europeans, Television New Zealand and Sky TV picked up the broadcasting rights, which at the time were owned by BMW New Zealand in conjunction with BMW Australia. There was a great deal of interest in this part of the world about what was going on in the UK. The BTCC was, at that time, one of the world's premier touring-car series, and thanks to both BMW companies we got to know the top drivers Paul was competing against in a series that became familiar to us.

Quite rightly, there was much excitement here about Paul heading off to Britain to compete, even if it wasn't for the first or even second time. This time he was in a highly regarded series and, best of all, he wasn't going to struggle financially or emotionally. There would be no need to go to Rob Whitehouse's office in South Kensington and beg to make a telephone call. His girlfriend did not need to sew the team's shirts nor stitch sponsor badges onto his racing overalls. For the first time in his life, he got his own flat, he bought a bed to sleep in, a table to eat at, and cutlery to eat with. It was such a novelty.

He was welcomed into both the Rouse family and into a team with good morale. The chief engineer was Vic Drake; the head mechanic was John Dorrans, a big, no-nonsense Northern Englishman whose son also worked in the team; and Paul's personal mechanic was Karl Williams. It was the nearest he had got to a family team since he'd left his own. He already knew Andy, his wife Sheila and their kids, and he soon got to know the team and their methods. Andy and Paul were similar in that neither of them were known as socialites or party-hoppers. They suited each other temperamentally off the track as much as they understood each other competitively.

To get a rapport with the team, I made sure I'd go there every day, talk with the guys and just sort of hang around. I wasn't trying to get in the way, but to understand everyone and get a relationship going.

His first official outing wasn't in a British Touring Car event nor even in one of the 2.0-litre cars, but in the much smaller super-mini class Fiesta. It was, in a sense, a test drive. Ford wanted to see Paul perform first-hand, so he headed to Oulton Park, just off the M20 in Kent, to pass his initiation test. He qualified third and won by a country mile, after which, he recalls, Ford felt a bit more relaxed about his abilities. And Paul was relaxed about himself — he was itching to get behind the wheel of the new Mondeo, even in the middle of an English winter.

This was Ford's first full-works entry into the British Touring Car Championships after the switch to the 2.0-litre formula in

1990, and Paul wanted to get the feel of what would become his office, to get some testing miles behind him, to learn the track well enough to move confidently into race mode for the first event, which was scheduled for March. It didn't quite happen like that.

Ford's decision to re-enter the British Touring Car Championship had come late in 1992, leaving Andy Rouse Engineering little time to develop the cars. They didn't receive the contract until the beginning of December, just three months before the start of the season. In fact, the Mondeo had not even gone into production and Ford wanted a year to develop the engines, which wasn't ideal for the race team. There was no alternative but for Rouse to build their initial development cars from two of Ford's pre-production test vehicles, and they did so within about five months.

The team knew that there was a problem with the weight of the car and, despite testing the suspension and chassis, they still couldn't seem to overcome heaviness with sheer speed. Out of frustration, Andy and engineer Vic Drake headed to the Ford plant in Genk, Belgium, and pored over the drawings. Seven special-order Mondeo Si bodyshells were constructed to Rouse's specification at the Belgium plant, while Cosworth was responsible for the race engines. Only four V6s were built for 1993, and these were to be shared between Paul and Andy. It left very little backup if one or more of them failed, so as a precautionary measure Cosworth planned to rebuild them for the team after just 800 running miles.

They rolled the Mondeos out for their first official appearance at a test session at Snetterton in early March. The cars came out

Paul (right, aged 8) and Chris (6) suited up in front of the family Triumph. Even at this age, both of them were quite capable of hopping into the driver's seat and taking command of the wheel — and would probably have done so with father Frank's blessing. RADISICH COLLECTION

By the time Paul was 10 he was dominating the Junior 125cc class in motocross. When he moved to the Senior 125cc class he was seeded in the top 10. He thought this was his career path until a crushed vertebra forced him to think there must be an easier way to race. RADISICH COLLECTION

Happy times together — the Radisich clan celebrating a family occasion. RADISICH COLLECTION

A look of concentration at 19 years old. His first single-seater drive came in the Ralt RT1 at Pukekohe. He qualified, but after that the car and the kid driver weren't going anywhere — the family needed car parts they couldn't find in time for the 1981 New Zealand Grand Prix.
TERRY MARSHALL

Two of the original Westie petrol-heads and members of the famous and extensive (if unofficial) 'Dally Mafia' that infiltrated motor racing from the early 'sixties. Robbie Francevic (left) and Frank Radisich (right).
RADISICH COLLECTION

Paul leading the bunch at Bay Park, Mt Maunganui. His fellow competitors didn't expect this to happen in just his second single-seater race. TERRY MARSHALL

The Datsun-powered RT1 in 1981, when the family and sponsors rallied around the young driver to give him some experience. TERRY MARSHALL

The original Zapata moustache has been trimmed, proving Paul Radisich was maturing off the track as well as on it.

Racing in the USA in 1988 in a team run by Dave Conti — the man some of the other Kiwis called 'The Rocket Scientist'. Paul won the Supervee race on the under-card for the US Grand Prix in Detroit. CHERYL DAY ANDERSON

Illustrious company indeed: Britain in 1987 — drivers who all went on to world recognition. From left: Damon Hill (UK), Maurizio Sandro-Sala (Brazil), and Hill's team-mate Paul Radisich (New Zealand).

The reigning World Touring Car Cup champion, in Britain in 1994 for his second year with Andy Rouse in British Touring Cars. RYO HAYASHIDA

Sir John Whitmore, the original 'kerb-hopper' of Britain. With form like this, he won the European Saloon Car Championship in 1965 in the Alan Mann Ford Lotus Cortina. Paul Radisich reintroduced the craft to Britain in 1993.
JOHN WHITMORE COLLECTION

Check-mate: Paul Radisich (left) attempts to check-mate Australian Mark Skaife (right). In fact it was a photo opportunity, and neither can play the game nearly as well as they each drive a race car. RADISICH COLLECTION

Frank, the frequent visitor to Australia during Paul's Dick Johnson Racing days, 2001. RADISICH COLLECTION

The Peugeot stint in British Touring Cars (1988) wasn't entirely successful, but the public relations exercise continued unabated. RADISICH COLLECTION

The unofficial Radisich fan club makes their feelings known in the UK. RADISICH COLLECTION

The fans speak. MARK HORSBURGH

Another day at the office. Paul returns to Pukekohe with considerable international experience on his CV.
RADISICH COLLECTION

Lucky to be alive after massive impact destroys the Team Kiwi Holden at the Bathurst 1000km race on 8 October 2006. MARK HORSBURGH

in rear-wheel-drive form, which surprised a number of people, because this configuration was never planned for production. Andy, however, believed the rear-drive Mondeo could offer superior on-track characteristics compared with the front-drive versions, despite having to contend with a 100kg penalty. He had latched on to a loophole in the rules that enabled a manufacturer that had a 4x4 version of the car to disconnect drive to either set of wheels and since a four-wheel-drive Mondeo was scheduled for manufacture in late 1993, Rouse took advantage of this clause.

By the end of April it was obvious that the cars were still well off the pace for a variety of reasons, only some of which could be traced to the series rules, and the pressure on Rouse to switch to a standard front-wheel-drive system was considerable. Their programme began to fall well behind schedule, but they had no option but to sit on the sidelines and work furiously to literally come up to speed. Paul could see his career heading for the skids before he'd even been given a chance to prove himself.

It was hard to sit it out, but I knew we didn't have a competitive car. At the same time, I was an unknown quantity and obviously not rated there as a driver. Yet if we'd gone out and been uncompetitive, I would have been written off, not the car.

In the end, it was a Ford production policy that forced the issue. The road-going Mondeo was selling so well that more had to be manufactured. Ford pushed back the production dates of its 4x4, which left the rear-drive cars ineligible for use in BTCC in

1993 and forced Rouse into switching the drive from the back to the front.

By this time, of course, all the other teams were acquiring data, experience and points. Andy at least had a working knowledge of all the tracks they would drive on, but Paul was starting cold for most of them, and there was nothing he could do to alter that. His ability to read a track quickly was going to be tried and tested. Luckily for him, his fellow competitors were unaware of this skill.

Finally, after seven races had passed them by over four rounds, when nearly half the championship had already come and gone, Andy Rouse, Paul Radisich and the team could get down to business in a front-wheel-drive Ford Mondeo.

The nightmare was over. The dream was just about to unfold.

Chapter 7

My part in the Battle of Britain

It took my fancy, I guess, to have this career, and then when it happened it was just, like, unbelievable!

After finally getting their act together, Andy Rouse Engineering and two Ford Mondeo cars driven by Andy Rouse from England and Paul Radisich from New Zealand showed up in front-wheel-drive form to a race at Pembrey Circuit in Carmarthenshire.

The airfield circuit was known at the time as the home of Welsh motor sport, and this was Ford's first chance all season to mount a fightback from nothing. In the seven races from four meetings that they had missed, the BMWs were dominating proceedings — but, really, every other car and driver in the entire field was in front of them at this point.

Paul had put pressure on himself and his capabilities during the prolonged development phase of the Mondeo programme, but there was additional responsibility that came with being an official works driver. He was the paid professional. The team was playing catch-up, and on top of that there was some subtle corporate pressure to make sure the Mondeo performed properly, meaning at the front end of the competition. An image had to be maintained, particularly on home soil and amongst invading 'foreigners'.

Ford had been extraordinarily successful in British Touring Cars in the preceding years, and it would have been disastrous for them to fail with their new car in front of a large English crowd and in full view of a worldwide television audience. No one had counted on them not performing at all, but at least they were now in the competition, albeit halfway through. For this reason alone they were guaranteed a certain amount of publicity. Paul finished a cautious eighth. Andy qualified fourth, but didn't finish. However, by the end of the day they knew that they had the hardware to get to the podium.

The next race on the calendar was at Silverstone, a track Paul knew well from his Formula 3 days, and, moreover, the race was one of the many supporting a Formula 1 event. No matter how much he was looking forward to getting out on the track, before the racing action started Paul had someone to meet. The Ford team were to receive a personal visit from HRH Princess Diana and her youngest son, Prince Harry, because, it was said, Harry was a Ford fan.

Every piece of chrome and bodywork was polished on the cars and polished again, so come Saturday we were gleaming. The Ford edict was specific: we were told how we should present ourselves and our person, and how we should greet the Royals.

We all lined up to greet the Princess; Andy Rouse

was first, and then the Princess came over to talk to me. She asked me whereabouts I came from in New Zealand, and asked about how the weekend was going, and wished me all the best before introducing Harry to me.

I signed some posters for Harry to take away.

During it all, the media scrum were falling all over themselves to get the best shot.

Not all of the 100,000-strong crowd at Silverstone that day were there to see the Royals, of course, or in fact Formula 1. British Touring Cars provided more action; they were the stock cars of Britain, and a lot more fun to watch than Formula 1. Paul qualified third and Andy was behind him in fourth.

We'd hardly got started when Jo Winkelhock and Steve Soper each gave me a huge serve, welcoming me to BTCC. I said to myself, 'I am not going to back down.'

When we finished, there wasn't one straight panel on the car. I finished third, and from there on I think I was accepted: I had passed my initiation test. It was almost as if they were saying, 'If you are going to play, you are going to play for keeps.'

It was my first time in the middle of it all, and I was surprised how aggressive it was. There was no quarter given, they would take any means to get by, but at the end it showed me I was one of them and not frightened to mix it up.

They were not boys to be toyed with. Soper in the Schnitzer BMW was vastly experienced, but so were others like Frenchman Alain Menu in the Renault, John Cleland and Jeff Allam in Vauxhalls, and Win Percy in the Nissan Primera. If Paul was going to mix it with these hard chargers, he had no alternative but to drive the same way as the rest of them.

It was probably the start of close racing and crashing and bashing, and you had to do that to survive, but because the races weren't particularly long and could be won or lost on the first lap, you had to be particularly aggressive to get through.

Looking back now I think it was too aggressive, but if you couldn't beat them you had to join them.

It was bloody tough, and yet Paul instinctively knew that the other professionals would climb all over him if he'd given way, so if that meant holding his line and banging a few doors, that's what had to happen. He made it clear that he was there to race, that he wasn't a 'dumb little Kiwi'. The stakes were high, both for himself and for Ford. Silverstone showed that the Mondeo was strong, possibly even a bit stronger than many of the other manufacturers' wares in the competition; it showed that Ford were podium contenders.

One of the people Paul beat that day was none other than the man who employed him, Andy Rouse. Most of the Brits who had raced against Andy and who knew his capabilities were staggered to think that a little Kiwi had lucked in sufficiently to trump a man of Rouse's talent. Paul who? Alan Gow, who had brokered the deal for Paul to drive with Rouse, never had any doubt that he would be competitive, but even he didn't reckon on the New Zealander beating the Englishman, especially so early in the piece.

The legendary Formula 1 commentator Murray Walker was covering both Formula 1 and BTCC, and was there for the podium presentation. He told Paul that he was impressed with his driving. The man famous for his 'muddly talker' comments produced one of his gems at a later race: 'The European drivers have adapted to this circuit extremely quickly, especially Paul Radisich, who is a New Zealander.'

It took Paul a couple of races (at Knockhill in Scotland, and Oulton Park in Cheshire) to settle into his stride, and his first win in the series came at Brands Hatch in Kent. It couldn't have come at a better time, because it gave Ford their 200th win in British Touring Cars. The company produced a large poster detailing every one of those 200 wins, with the Kiwi's name rounding out their achievements.

There is a suggestion (mostly from New Zealanders, it has to be said) that Paul was the first touring-car driver in Britain to deliberately kerb-hop, to place two wheels on the candy-striped 'humps' on the side of the track in order to gain a momentum advantage. The other drivers, even the hardened European professionals, didn't race like this, but in fact a precedent had been set in the UK in the 1960s. Sir John Whitmore was a European and British saloon-car champion and he didn't just hit the ripple strip in his Lotus Cortina, he aimed for the six-inch-high kerb at some tracks.

> *I realized that if I could get the wheel up high enough I could hang it up in the air on top of the kerb and in doing so I could straighten out the road. The trick was that you couldn't possibly afford to make a mistake, because it's an absolutely vertical kerbstone, and if you hit that you'd break the front suspension or throw the car over. You had to get the wheel up as high as you could.*

To his way of thinking, ripple strips were kindergarten kerbs.

Many years later, Peter Brock did something similar Down Under, and Paul remembers watching him around the streets of Wellington in 1990 in the Sierra Cosworth.

> *I was happily driving around Wellington in my Sierra when suddenly Peter Brock came screaming by me in his Sierra, with his wheels bouncing all over the place, up against the walls on two wheels. Wellington was so bumpy, but Brocky could drive the thing so hard, and I remember thinking 'So that's how you drive a touring car!'*
>
> *It isn't until you follow someone in another car that you learn a lot more, and at that time the Sierras*

were pretty uncouth — all that horsepower on skinny tyres — but he was showing me how it could be done. So straight away I started to drive like that and to change my driving style to be a lot more aggressive. I got down and drove the cars properly and I went faster, too.

Whether Paul introduced these tactics to British Touring Cars in the 1990s is open to dispute: other drivers are loath to concede a point, either on or off the track. There is no doubt, though, that like Sir John Whitmore in the Ford Lotus Cortina, Paul was assisted by his Ford, the Mondeo. The front-drive 2.0-litre vehicles were still undergoing a gestation period, and Andy was one of the first to develop the car's shock absorbers. The Mondeo could essentially float over the kerbs, and Paul took full advantage of that.

One technique he did excel at was left-foot braking. When he arrived from New Zealand, Paul found that most of the saloon-car drivers in Europe braked with their right foot. When Paul, however, would head up the hill at the tight Thruxton circuit with his foot still on the throttle and his left foot on the brake at the same time, some of the other drivers began to ask themselves what this was all about. Once they had figured out what he was doing, a few of the more enterprising drivers booked into Pentti Airikkala's race-and-rally school at Silverstone to get the 1989 RAC Rally winner to teach them the art of left-foot braking, in the hope that they could not only emulate Paul, but beat him at his own game.

Most of the top drivers in the British Touring Car Series were being paid; they didn't have any of their own money in the team, and so they felt quite comfortable with some reasonably aggressive racing tactics — after all, they didn't have to pay for any damaged panels. This led to some interesting encounters out on the track, such as the one in a TOCA shoot-out at Donington at the end of the year. Before the race, Jeff Allam and John Cleland had agreed between themselves that whoever won the race would split the prize money with the other, so they would get £10,000 each. At one point in the race, Jeff had an imposing lead with John Cleland behind him when one Mr Radisich appeared in their mirrors in third place in the Mondeo. Jeff recalls it as if it were yesterday:

> *Paul followed us for a lap, then came down to the hairpin. I was minding my own business when I saw Cleland pull over to block him. The Mondeo had a front bumper on it built like an Irish drain, and suddenly Paul used Cleland as a brake, which made him slam into me, which made me under-steer into the corner allowing Paul to sneak through!*
>
> *He obviously knew that the front bumper was strong when he whacked John. I couldn't believe it, but I didn't get the red mist like John, who was fuming.*

John went hunting for Paul in *parc fermé*, but Jeff suspects that Paul ran away before he could be reached. That's one side of the story. Paul didn't know these things were being played out in John Cleland's mind — he was busy doing media duty because he'd won. 'By the time he put on his kilt he probably calmed down, and he would have saved his retribution in his sporran for another day.'

At Brands Hatch, Jeff had another encounter with Paul. Allam was sitting in sixth place when Paul came up behind him, gave him a tap in the rear and spat him across the track towards the barrier on the other side. One of the big Volvo Estates missed him by inches and he still doesn't know how he wasn't collected, and, as he says, it was one of his mates dealing to him! 'I was not happy with young Paul that day. I was not happy at all.'

If there wasn't much love lost between any of the drivers on the track, it was quite a different matter off it. In contrast to other European classes, the drivers in this series tended to socialize *après* race. There was an unusually high degree of camaraderie between drivers, mechanics, partners, children, and all the extended families, replicating the 'good old days' in motor sport, the days before the 1980s, when these things were considered the norm.

Paul began to consolidate his presence. He won by a massive 10 seconds in the wet at Donington, and won again at Silverstone a few weeks later. He had pushed the Mondeo from the workshop to reasonably regular podium places within the space of a few months, and in the process was consistently outshining his team boss, a former multiple winner of the British Touring Car Championship. A second-string driver wasn't meant to do that! It could have caused friction between the two men, but the only time they ever had words about driving tactics was at Donington when Andy got the better start and Paul charged up the inside and worked him out of the way. For the majority of their events, they consciously worked as a team.

'Andy would protect my lead if I had it and he would tail me for a few laps to make sure it stayed that way and to give me some breathing space.'

Andy Rouse is the first to admit that he and Paul are different drivers and that they used different techniques, left-foot braking being one of them.

> *His left-foot braking was good for all the tight corners. He was harsh on brakes, hard on the equipment, and we just had to build him a strong car.*
>
> *The other part of his technique was the shortcuts he took. He'd come in with square wheels because he'd been driving over the kerbs, and he set a new style of touring-car driving. The good thing was that the Mondeo was good for that — with the dampers and all the suspension, we made the car able to ride up the kerbs, and this was a major part of the success. We used to get through about three spoilers a meeting, too, but we were happy he was up the front.*

The Mondeo also benefited from a change of tyres. Vic Drake, the Rouse Team chief engineer, says they were constantly 'cooking' the Yokohamas. He and Paul discussed using Michelins, yet Andy didn't want to change brands. At Silverstone (after Paul's first podium finish), they were approached by a representative from the French company and took the car out for a test at Pembrey with a set of Michelins in place. 'Straightaway they were quick, and they seemed reasonably durable. The guys tuned the car to suit the tyres, and we went back to the workshop and decided we had to have them. From that point onwards we were competitive, and that's when we started to dominate.'

The team thus introduced Michelin to British Touring Cars, but even so Paul believes that those tyres worked better on the Mondeo than on any of the other car brands in the series at that point.

With Paul rapidly asserting his authority on the track in England, Frank and Robyn slugged out the air miles from New Zealand to see him race from time to time, but they were not officially part of the team. They'd learned to stand back a little over the preceding few years, and to let other team managers and engineers do their thing. On those occasions they'd generally been tipping money into the coffers and felt they had a right to an opinion, even if those team managers and engineers didn't always agree with it. This time in Britain it was a novelty to be 'just' parents.

To make them feel more at home in the first year when they weren't at the track, Paul generously allowed them to paint his house, and in between times Alan Gow became their tour guide, providing them with a learned commentary on the history of various towns, Winchester Cathedral, Warwick Castle, and other places of interest. Robyn says that if he hadn't been so big-hearted neither she nor Frank would have seen anything other than the inside of a race track or the back end of a paint pot.

Alan was the head of the British Touring Car Championship at the time, and there were some questions about whether or not Paul had favoured status with the Australian. Fellow competitor (and later team-mate) Tim Harvey says he is simply 'not convinced' that it didn't occur, and points out that Alan was Paul's manager.

Certainly Alan was acting as a mentor to Paul at that time — he still is today — but Paul says that when he was driving in British Touring Cars their relationship more often than not worked to his disadvantage, noting that Alan went to considerable lengths not to be seen to show this closeness. In fact, there were many times when he felt as if Alan's reluctance to intervene hindered him.

> *I used to get mad at Alan and say to him, 'I know we're buddies', and he'd say that it doesn't get in the way and that he couldn't be seen to let it get in the way. But I think Alan sometimes made it harder for me because of our association. I'd approach him about it and he would say, 'Bullshit, you're talking out of your arse.'*
>
> *I think some of the other drivers would give him a hard time behind the scenes, saying he was favouring me, but that was totally not the case. They would also wind him up, which they knew they could do. Alan Gow doing favours for someone? Unheard of!*

Twice, Alan Gow and Paul Radisich have together faced what they call near-death experiences. The first came in the 1980s when they were returning from the Sandown circuit near Melbourne and a car zoomed out from a side-street towards them. Alan recalls:

I wrenched the wheel and spun around in front of this car, and if it hadn't have been for that we would have been T-boned and injured at best, or at worst we would have died. We just sat there and looked at each other, didn't say a word, and then breathed.

The second occasion was in England, on a road between Leamington Spa and Silverstone that a few of the local boys (like Andy Rouse) had told them about. The road was generally only used by farmers, and Paul and Alan took the route to avoid traffic.

It's a fantastic road and Paul was driving. We were going flat-out as usual — and came around a corner to see a tractor sitting in the middle of the road. Paul had to jam on everything to try to stop in time. The car went up the bank, touched the side, skidded along on two wheels and scraped past the tractor.

We could have been history and how he managed that I'll never know. Once again we just sat there and looked at each other.

Amazingly, given their racing experience, neither of them was wearing a seat belt. Somewhat less traumatic was the skirmish they had when they were out 'jogging': Paul was running while Alan was riding a little motorized ride-on scooter to help him keep fit. Alan hit a kerb and went sailing over the handlebars, injuring his arm and leg. Paul laughed like a drain as Alan was lying in one.

At the end of his first season in the British Touring Car Championship, Paul finished the series in third place, behind the BMWs of Germany's Joachim Winkelhock and England's Steve Soper. In 10 races, Paul had three wins, two fastest laps and two pole positions. It was a remarkable effort, considering the hesitant start and the fact he had really only been able to get into his stride when the series was halfway through. Andy Rouse finished 11th.

All this was achieved on what was tantamount to a clerk's wages. He and Alan were sharing the first year's salary, but at that stage Paul didn't care a whit, because for the first time in his life someone was paying him to go motor racing for an entire year.

By then, Paul knew he had a good car, he had got to know the team, he had competed on nearly all the tracks in the series, and he was settling in to his new English environment. He knew he was the equal of, and at times superior to, the top touring-car drivers in the world. With these things in mind, he prepared to go to Italy to contest the first of the World Touring Car Cup races at Monza.

He had plenty of support there, but in retrospect it's a shame Frank and Robyn didn't make another trip. If only they had known what was coming up.

Chapter 8

Sitting on top of the world

There was a time in my life when I viewed touring cars as something I wouldn't get satisfaction from.

In the northern autumn of 1993, Paul flew to Monza in Italy, but not for a holiday; he was there to race. And not just any old race: a world title was at stake.

Italy's third-largest city sits on the River Lambro and is best known for its Grand Prix circuit — the Autodromo Nazionale Monza — and as the home of Alfa Romeo. The circuit is fast, often full-throttle and mostly flat, but with a notable elevated gradient so steep that *Autosport* suggests that it is a blasé person indeed who can walk by without stopping to marvel at the thought of cars racing on it. It is the spiritual home of the Scuderia Ferrari, and those most ardently passionate of all motor-racing fans, the *tifosi*.

Of course, Paul knew the history of the place and could feel it when he visited the museum and merchandise lane, but for a boy brought up Down Under, Bathurst held much more mystique, so he wasn't overawed by the Italian track's reputation. The wine-drinking *tifosi*, however, might be considered marginally more sophisticated than the XXXX-drinking mob on McPhillamey Park.

There were Supertouring championships held in a number of countries by 1993. The concept of uniting the best of those in one event was initiated by Alan Gow, although a precedent had been established in 1987, but as a series, not a single event. This had been started by a New Zealander, the late Ian Gamble (the man who orchestrated the Wellington street race), and was sanctioned by the world governing body for motor sport, the FIA. It was won by Italian Roberto Ravaglia in a BMW M3, but after only one year it was dissolved, the blame falling on the high costs of maintaining it and the cars.

The one-off World Touring Car Cup event in Italy, again sanctioned by the FIA, was designed to pitch the top drivers and manufacturers from the Supertouring countries against each other. Each manufacturer involved would be represented by three cars and three drivers, who could be selected from any of the participating countries. This meant Paul had a problem.

New Zealand didn't have a team in the race, and Paul, of course, is a New Zealander. Moreover, the event required that contestants should be either champions or runners-up, and he didn't qualify in this department either, because he'd been third in the BTCC championship. Discussions flew backwards and forwards between Europe and England, and it wasn't until just a week before the event was to be run that he was given the OK to fly to Monza.

The grid featured 50 cars in the hands of some of the best touring-car drivers in the world, some of whom had raced Down

Under and others whom we had seen only on television. The names had that superstar ring around them: Tarquini, Giovanardi, Soper, Ravaglia, Larini, Winkelhock. Even ex-Formula 1 drivers Emmanuele Pirro and Stefano Modena had been especially hooked in to the event by Alfa Romeo, which was competing on home turf and ploughing a considerable amount of time, effort and money into the event. They were, according to Andy Rouse, spending about 10 times the budget of his team. Even so, the Mondeo was the form car, and there were high expectations that Paul would be competitive.

From the first lap I realized that Monza suited our car; there was a lot of top-end stuff available, so I knew the car would be fairly good. It was a fairly easy track to learn, but I didn't shine in the practice sessions. I was somewhere near the top but not right there.

Qualifying is more important than winning at that stage, and — to the amazement of a number of people, particularly the Europeans who knew he wasn't familiar with the track — Paul grabbed pole position. Next to him was Nicola Larini, who was in an Alfa Romeo on his home track. To the Italians the almost impossible had happened, with the potential for the unthinkable to occur.

The other drivers were being paid enormous amounts of money to drive, some at least £250,000. In contrast, Paul was on secretary's wages. He considered himself to be the cheapest driver in the world, and there he was, sitting in the number-one slot.

All of the drivers were representing their country and the manufacturer of their choice; each and every manufacturer was striving for attention; the *tifosi* were backing everything Italian; and the whole lot was to be televised around the world. There was a great deal of pride on the line, and the first race lasted one lap. A multi-car pile-up, which involved Andy Rouse, meant that the race had to be aborted. Paul was reasonably happy with this, because he'd had a bad start and had found himself in third place by the first corner. A restart meant he could redeem himself. Second time around, he got the start he wanted.

Throughout the first race he held his lead and, as much as one can in a motor race, he increasingly looked like he would win. But this was Italy. The race was being controlled by Italian officials and, with the Alfa Romeos trailing behind the Ford, the pace car was brought out in the dying stages of the race to close up the gap.

The pace car stayed out there for the last two laps, so it ended up being a dash to the finish and I managed to hold them off. I must say it was really satisfying being able to beat Alfa in their own back yard.

Frenchman Alain Cudini was second in an Opel Vectra, and Nicola Larini in the Alfa 155 was third. Alfa Romeo promptly protested the Rouse team, claiming that the front spoiler was too low. Vic Drake, the Rouse team engineer, pointed out that since Paul had been kerb-hopping (again) the spoiler was smashed to smithereens, so how, he argued, could it be too low? The officials accepted his reasoning, and Paul started the second race from pole.

It had rained between the two races, and to make life more interesting only half the field was on wet tyres. Vic Drake thought the track would dry.

> *We grabbed four bedded slicks and put them on the trolley. I told the team to stick them on, and told Paul to be careful for the first few laps. With about three laps to go, he was in the lead by about eight seconds and there was a minor incident, so the Italians, being Italian, put the safety car out.*
>
> *I said to Paul over the radio that the lights were off, so at Parabolica he came around leading the pack and stood on the brakes. The pack slowed down. He sped up a bit, put on the brakes again, and then suddenly put his foot down and crossed the start line ahead of everyone else!*

By taking victory in both races, Paul claimed a world title for himself, for Ford, for Britain, for the Rouse team — and for New Zealand. Since he was the only New Zealander participating in the event, he earned enough points all on his own to give his country third place in the teams event, behind Italy and France, both of which were represented by two drivers. In a sense, it was a Commonwealth victory, and for Vic Drake, who had engineered the car, for 'Britain' to have beaten the Italians in an Italian car marked one of his proudest moments. 'To beat the Italians in

Italy is an achievement, because they always try to keep you out and they cheat so much, so it was the best race ever when Paul won!'

Alan Gow remembers hearing 'Radis...eeeech' in a frenzy over the PA system dozens of times, especially when he made his way to the podium for the presentation. 'I was standing at the bottom of the podium and saw Paul going up to the top step. I was thinking how bizarre it all was. Twelve months ago there was no touring car world event, and here was my little mate winning the thing. It was a fairy tale.' He had tears in his eyes.

Paul, on the other hand, was standing on the podium without any emotion other than sheer relief that it was all over.

> *It was a really tough event to win. I'd had a good lead in the second event, and I sort of expected the Italians to do something, because there was a string of Alfas behind me, and they did — they brought out the pace car.*
>
> *It meant there had to be this huge amount of concentration: I couldn't relax anywhere and every corner was a different scenario.*
>
> *And because it had been a wet and dry race, you had to be really vigilant just dealing with the elements.*

Rob Whitehouse, the man who had financially mentored Paul into Formula 3 for his second season in 1986, was by this time living in Barbados. He had managed to go to the BTCC race at Silverstone, where Paul paid him back, as it were, by achieving his first podium. Rob was so excited at the prospect of a world event that he'd turned up at Monza without even having a hotel room booked. The place was so full that he ended up sharing with Paul. At the track he went to the chicane to get a good look.

> *It was really close racing, and Paul was hitting those kerbs so violently I couldn't believe it, but he kept his head under tremendous pressure. The second race he won relatively easily. I was immensely proud. I made my way back to the pits and I heard something familiar over the PA. I thought to myself, 'I know that tune, I've heard it somewhere before.' And then I remembered. It was the national anthem of New Zealand!*

Rob managed to sneak into the press conference. Nicola Larini from the Alfa Romeo team had recently been crowned the German Touring Car Champion, and had expected to beat Ford and this virtually unknown driver from New Zealand. He was so miffed at not winning in an Italian car on his home ground that he obstinately refused to answer questions in anything but Italian. Paul said no one asked him anything about New Zealand, because the conference was being conducted by the Italians, who had hung their hat on being competitive in touring cars and hadn't won. So far as they were concerned, they had been beaten by a Brit in a British car and it simply should not have happened.

But it had, and Paul had become the first World Touring Car Cup title-holder. He was delighted and the team were ecstatic. They and all the Ford representatives present headed to dinner that evening in the old Monza township, and as they entered the pizza restaurant all the diners and the entire staff gave them a standing ovation.

Back home in New Zealand during the very early hours of the morning, Robyn and Frank Radisich climbed out of bed in Turua to take a telephone call from their son. They had always been very confident of Paul's ability on the race track, and knew he just needed the right opportunity at the right time. He had delivered: a world title at last.

There was considerable respect back in the UK for Paul's achievement, even if, as some members of the media pointed out, he wasn't bulldog British. They circumvented his accident of birth by calling him an Honorary Brit, and somewhat ruefully acknowledged that he was the best of the British team, who'd collectively had a miserable day overall. Then inevitably the question was asked: how had he done it?

The equation was relatively straightforward. Take one highly competitive driver with years of international racing experience in both single-seaters and touring cars, add in a very strong car with the slippery shape entirely suited to the fast Monza circuit, and you get two races and two victories. Of course, there was an element of luck involved, as there is in any race, but Paul says that on that day he really did feel at one with the car and the track.

Every manufacturer present had spent thousands trying to achieve that one title alone, with the Italians spending the most. Moreover, Alfa Romeo had had the advantage of being able to test on the circuit long before any of the other teams arrived, and they still hadn't won. Australia had sent over Mark Skaife, who at that time was driving for Nissan, so in Italy he drove a Primera. He ended up punting off his team-mate, Keith Odor, in the warm-up lap, which was not, says Alan Gow, the brightest thing to do on a world stage.

Paul headed home to England a very happy man, and when he got to his house the sitting room was awash with fax paper. He'd had so many calls on the phone/fax that the roll had spewed out across the floor, and to this day he doesn't know how everyone managed to get his number.

The enormous amount of media attention kept Paul busy for days. He had arranged for the Mondeo and some of the Rouse team to travel to New Zealand to show people there what it was all about, and the timing of this trip meant he couldn't attend the official FIA awards ceremony, which was to be held in Monaco. As a result, and somewhat forlornly, the trophy was mailed to Andy Rouse's workshop. Trophy or not, Paul was out to show his countrymen how it was done, and so he entered the Nissan Mobil Series. Vic Drake headed his technical team:

We took five lads out with us, and when we arrived in New Zealand we discovered that Paul was a real hero. When we came through the airport in Auckland, everyone knew him and I got an upgrade because of him!

Australian Glenn Seton partnered Paul for the race series. Paul put the car on pole in Wellington and drove the first leg; but during his stint Seton ended up putting the Mondeo into the wall by the harbour, because the wind was blowing the spray onto the circuit and it caught him unawares. A week later at Pukekohe, Paul set the fastest lap of the day and won the race by about four laps, which allowed him and Seton to win the series.

Paul flew back to Britain for another season to try to capture the British Touring Car Championship title, which had eluded him in the first season. He wasn't short of options; he'd had an offer from BMW to change stripes, but he decided to remain loyal to Ford — and Ford certainly wanted him to stay.

He also needed to defend his World Touring Car Cup title, which, according to many pundits, would be well-nigh impossible. In the five months between seasons, the competition in BTCC had become considerably tougher.

Chapter 9

Not goodbye, but *au revoir*

The whole emphasis changed from trying to get there, struggling for a lifetime, scraping through, and I thought, 'Gee, what do I do now?' That was probably one of the biggest things to start coping with.

G oing into his second season in British Touring Cars there were high expectations on the Rouse team, and on Paul Radisich in particular, to continue their world-title form and to improve on the third place they'd obtained in the championship in 1993. But somewhere along the way the season became more of a struggle than they imagined it would. Controlled tyres had been brought in and, although the Rouse teams opted for Michelins again, the restrictions meant that they were no longer entirely suited to the Mondeo. It didn't help that the ante had been well and truly upped by the other manufacturers.

Volvo elected to run what the Brits call an 'estate car', or a station wagon, and there were a few guffaws huffed up people's sleeves at this decision. The 1994 season also introduced Walkinshaw, Renault and Williams to the championship, and a Formula 1-style approach to touring cars was starting to creep in. The signing of Gabriele Tarquini and Giampiero Simoni to the Alfa Romeo team, with a reported budget of £6 million, was a prime example of how things had 'progressed'. National pride and internecine rivalry comes at a price, and in 1994 everyone found themselves spending a lot more. In addition to the struggle on the track, there was also more personal pressure on Paul himself.

You go from doing the chasing to being the person who is being chased, and you have to admire people like Michael Schumacher, who can rally around and get people behind him to be able to stay there at the top.

Andy ran the team and he was the engineer along with Vic Drake, and, as far as the set up of the car goes, that was my affair and I did what I had to do with what I had.

Paul was consistently up the front in the first part of races, but the car had a tendency to fade towards the end. Part of the problem could be traced to the tyres, but that wasn't the only issue; some of the other competitors were also using Michelins.

The Mondeo had been practically bulletproof in the first season, and quite rightly Andy Rouse believed that he had a superior car. He seemed to work on the assumption that if it wasn't broke, it didn't need fixing. The other manufacturers, however, were heavily into development. Gabriele Tarquini in the Alfa Romeo was very quick indeed, and Paul clearly remembers John Cleland in the Vauxhall:

*In one race I had such a big lead over John Cleland
that he looked like a dot back in the distance, but by
halfway my front tyres were shot and I ended up having
to nurse the car home. It was the start of Vauxhall's
evolution — it was lightweight and the Mondeo was
heavy — and the next thing John would come by really
quickly.*

The Vauxhalls, he says, appeared to be 'supersonic', and it didn't
do much for his morale, especially as he'd been earmarked as
the one to watch at the beginning of the season. Andy Rouse
tried to convince Ford to put more money into a development
programme, but Ford were reluctant to commit to this. They were
trying to save beans not plant them, and in the meantime other
drivers and manufacturers were surging ahead.

*I had gone from chasing to being chased and I thought,
how the hell do I stay there? I found it hard to deal
with, because I was expected to win, and when I didn't
I didn't cope with it very well. As time went on, that
frustration showed on the track. Over a period of time,
things went backwards. It's one thing to be chasing
your goals; it's quite another how you maintain it.*

At one point Paul called the Mondeo a bucket of bolts, which
totally bemused engineer Vic Drake, because he had just won a
race. Some of the team questioned Paul's attitude, feeling that he
wasn't trying to get as much out of himself as he had in the past.

As engineers, they may have been looking for an opportunity to pin the lack of performance on someone or something out of their control. In reality, though, the car development just wasn't there. Was the boss, Andy Rouse, stuck in a groove? While other manufacturers were wind-tunnel testing, he would cast his engineer's eye over a chassis and say it looked 'about right'. He appeared not to be keeping pace, and the Ford Motor Company became as frustrated as the drivers. But without more financial input, to at least match that of Vauxhall, for example, Andy's cars weren't surging ahead.

The driving standard didn't help matters. It was *de rigueur* to bang doors, cut corners, wreck tyres, brakes and panels — and that was just practising safety-car procedures in a road car! Some manufacturers were replacing the team's road cars every couple of months. Imagine the cost of panel damage to a race car when the spoilers alone cost around £12,000 apiece.

There was a consolation win for Paul over Alain Menu at Silverstone, but the biff and bang continued both on and off the track. At Oulton Park, officials told the Alfa team to remove their aero package. They refused, packed up, and went home in a huff. They failed to race at the next round, which cut Tarquini's sizeable points lead in the series. They reappeared at Donington with their wings literally clipped, and were slower than the Fords and the Vauxhalls. It was one of those seasons, and — although Paul may have had trouble with tyres and have worried about the weight of the car compared with that of the other contenders — heading into the last rounds he was second in the championship.

We had expected to come out and continue where we had left off, but that wasn't the case. We won a few races and Cosworth were trying to get more performance out of the engine, and at the last round I should have finished runner-up in the competition. But my engine let go, Alain Menu came past me and got a couple of points to finish second in the series, so all in all it was a very disappointing season, even though third is good. I'd expected to dominate. We all had.

Gabriele Tarquini in the Alfa Romeo won the championship, and Andy Rouse finished 11th again, this time equal with Julian Bailey.

Once again, at the end of the season they prepared for another World Touring Car event, this time to be held at the Donington circuit in the Midlands in England; and this time, of course, Paul had a title to defend.

I remember going out in the first practice session, and as I was going down the Craner Curves — which is the fastest part of the track — I had this feeling of confidence, and I remember saying to myself: 'I have won this event.'

For the first race, he thought he was back in Italy. He got pole but didn't get a good start, and because of an incident further down the pack the race was red-flagged early on. In fact, on both occasions (at Monza and at Donington) the race director was

Australian Tim Schenken, who probably doesn't realize to this day the enormous favour he gifted Paul by halting both races in their early stages. At Donington, Paul again got a better start the second time around.

He was in the lead with seven car lengths on Steve Soper when, with about 10 laps to go, the sequential gearbox started giving him trouble.

I was panicking a bit because I could see the lead being reduced, and I didn't want to lose the race because of a mechanical issue, so I radioed across to the team. They couldn't do anything about it, but I had to tell them.

Over in the pits, Vic Drake was worried as well, because he thought Paul would stop somewhere down the back of the track.

We all thought: mass panic! We had a system where the engine would cut for a fraction of a second to make the gear slide in more easily, and we thought it had packed up. But it wasn't actually the current race that Paul was thinking about: he was talking about the winner-take-all £20,000 race, and he was telling us to get it sorted for that!

The second race that day — the one that Paul had radioed the team about with such concern — was the TOCA shoot-out. The format was based on Britain's oldest race, the TT. The fastest car (which was Paul) would start at the back. After 10 laps, the slowest car at the back would stop. Some of the World Cup contenders decided not to enter because they thought it was too much of a gimmick, but the prize money kept many others interested. For the second time that day (or the third if you count the restart in the first race), Paul lined up on the grid.

It is quite a good format and you have to judge it right so you aren't the last car. I had a big battle with John Cleland and Jeff Allam, but in the end we got to the front and I crossed the line in first.

Against the odds, Paul won the World Touring Car Cup for the second time. He captured another world title, and he did so in Britain in a British car, the equivalent of which Alfa Romeo had not been able to achieve in Italy. They hadn't even won in Britain. There was an awful lot for Paul, the team, and Britain to be thrilled about.

He received a percentage of the prize money, and this time it was made very clear by the FIA that he had to go to Monaco to receive his trophy. It was hardly a difficult task, of course, and, because the FIA wanted his car there as well, the Rouse boys packed it up in the transporter and drove it to the Hôtel de Paris on the Monte Carlo waterfront. Not only would Paul be there, but so too would world champions of the sport from all over the world. It was motor racing's equivalent of the Oscars; a black-tie, red-carpet occasion.

The Hôtel de Paris, where the awards ceremony was to be

conducted and where Paul stayed, had been built in 1864 to exemplify the privileged and monied aura of the tiny principality. It has first-class views to the Mediterranean, and next-door is the famed Casino. During the afternoon before the ceremony, Paul slipped down the road to have a quiet cup of coffee.

There were Bentleys and Ferraris all around the place, and I watched this young dude rock up in his open-top Ferrari and pull into a parking spot. There was a Ferrari in front of him and a Porsche behind him, and he nudged the one in front and nudged the one at the back trying to negotiate his way into a tight spot, and then put up his hand and said, 'Sorry!'

Everyone in the café clapped him. It is a different world. It's not a real world but it was great to have a very short time there and be part of it.

Before the function started, Paul mingled outside in the square and was fascinated, bemused and not a little in awe of the parade of famous faces swirling around him. He became inwardly excited when Michael Schumacher passed by, forgetting for a moment that he, too, was a world champion in his own right.

Paul wasn't the only New Zealander attending the awards function that night in Monaco. Possum Bourne had won the Asia Pacific Rally Championship with Subaru and was there with his wife Peggy. The rally man from Pukekohe and the circuit racer from West Auckland were mentally pinching themselves — they were in Monte Carlo with the best of the best, drivers, teams, manufacturers, those at the very top of their game, their profession.

Paul received his trophy from Formula 1's supreme head, Bernie Ecclestone, with the President of the FIA, Max Mosley, also in attendance. He was on a world stage, all black décor and swirling smoke.

The whole ceremony was in French and I couldn't understand it, but then I heard 'Radiseeeeeech' . . . and everyone clapped. I took a bow and that was it! Bernie said congratulations and said he had followed the touring cars a little bit and that I had success so quickly.

I said I would have really liked to play in his game, and he laughed and made some comment about, well, maybe . . .

It was pretty awesome to be there.

Paul may have been competing for a British team in a car entered by Ford of Britain, but at that precise moment he was most certainly a Kiwi.

Did these two world titles change him? There are some who say no, he was just the same old Paul from New Zealand who remained the polite person he always was. The New Zealand public, the media, and his family certainly thought that. But there are those who suggest that he let some of the adulation go to his head. With his tongue somewhat in his cheek, Alan Gow says that he thought Paul became a 'bit of a smart-arse', and because of that he couldn't find quite the teary-eyed emotion at Donington that he had at Monza. Paul, naturally enough, isn't sure that's entirely correct.

After the World Cup it was like I was instantly flavour of the month, but I had spent 10 or 12 years trying to get a direction. I know people say I changed, and I probably did a little bit, but that was just me coping with the instant success and the demands on my time when I had not been used to all of that.

Not everyone, however, saw his victory as the ultimate achievement. Andy Rouse and Vic Drake believe that Paul's attitude to the car changed after his second title win. In their opinion, Paul felt that he no longer had to improve himself, because he was a double world champion. He became, in their eyes, far more ready to blame the car for any non-performance.

Paul gave some of the prize money to some of the 'lads' in the team and gave his crash helmet to another. To this day, Vic Drake appears to be a little bitter about not receiving anything personally, but Paul did send a case of wine to the Rouse Engineering workshop.

Back in New Zealand, Paul was a finalist in the Halberg Sportsman of the Year Award 1994. He was up against Danyon Loader (swimming), Mark Rendell (cycling), and Vaughan Jefferis (equestrian) for the men's award, and of course the supreme award.

In the end none of the men captured the top prize, which

went to double scullers Philippa Baker and Brenda Lawson, who, like Paul, had won their first world title in 1993. Up until then, the only other motor-racing person (excluding motorcycling) to be recognized by the Halberg Awards was Denny Hulme, who took the supreme title in 1967 after he won the World Formula 1 championship.

Paul, his family and, indeed, New Zealand had every reason to be proud. He had served his time, he had paid his dues, and he now had two world titles to his credit. Unfortunately, that success wasn't to last.

A year is a long time in motor racing.

Andy Rouse made the decision to retire from active driving at the end of 1994 to concentrate more on the business side of the sport. He needed to replace himself in the team for the 1995 season and he chose a British driver to do so. Birmingham-born Kelvin Burt had come up through the classic motor-racing ranks before becoming a test driver with the Jordan Formula 1 team, and he became available for the 1995 season when Jordan didn't take up his option.

As the 1995 season progressed, the team thought the Cosworth engines were down on horsepower compared with the previous year. Ironically, although Cosworth were paid well by Ford, Andy Rouse points out that the engines were slower that season. But they couldn't do much about it, since Ford was pushing cost-cutting down their necks and had brought in Australian company man Peter Gillitzer to wield the guillotine. Despite this, there was still pressure on Paul to keep up front.

'Once things start rolling you want to keep it going. We would have flashes of being at the front, but we couldn't keep it going on a consistent basis.'

There was something of a season high point, however, when Nigel Mansell joined the team for a one-off appearance at Donington — and along with him came the fans. In the UK, Nigel was considered god-like, and over 100,000 turned up to see the former World Formula 1 and IndyCar champion in the Mondeo. 'Both Nigel and I had a police escort to the event from our hotel, there was such utter Mansell mania, with fans mobbing the cars and the press hunting us down.'

Nigel had asked Paul to give him some touring-car driving instructions prior to the event, but in the race he totally destroyed the car in a massive shunt. Still, if all publicity is good publicity, Ford got some of the best they'd had all season. The team were featured on television and in the papers before the event, and Mansell's spectacular accident made the media for days afterwards. Some of the bits off his car were later sold at a charity auction. Paul says that he thoroughly enjoyed meeting Nigel and being his team-mate, however brief their time together.

If the team felt frustrated at their lack of track progress, then so did Paul. According to Vic Drake, one incident, more than the engineering problems perhaps, seemed to take some of the stuffing out of the New Zealander. At the appropriately named Knockhill circuit in Scotland, Vauxhall team driver James Thompson had a horrific 100-kph accident at the infamous Duffus Dip during testing, which put him out of the series for the remainder of the season. Before his own race the next day, Paul went to visit James in hospital, and found him sitting up in bed but with his eyes so bruised that he looked like a panda. Vic believes Paul was never quite the same on the track all season thereafter. Paul disagrees; he thinks that Vic's interpretation of what happened may have been an excuse for the car not working well.

At season's end, Paul and Kelvin finished sixth and eighth in the championship, respectively, and crossed the Channel to France, heading for the Paul Ricard circuit near Nice for the third World Touring Car Cup event. There, they faced more problems. They were using the Michelins that had served them so well in previous cup title events, but this time Michelin chose to give Rouse's tyres to BMW, suggesting to the Ford team that they simply didn't have enough to go around.

Cosworth supposedly had a new, demon-tweak engine for the Paul Ricard event, and the team's instructions from Ford were to wait until Peter Gillitzer arrived before putting it in one of the cars. He turned up late, and the boys had to scramble around at the last minute to install the engine in time. Tellingly, they put it into Kelvin Burt's car. Paul had no idea that the 'standard' engine they were replacing was, in fact, the special Cosworth engine. In the end, German driver Frank Biela won the event in an Audi A4 Quattro, and Ford put the works' touring-car contract up for auction.

In between seasons, Paul shot back Down Under and teamed up with young Auckland driver Nigel Arkell to campaign a Ford Telstar in the New Zealand Touring Car Championship in a team run by Neil Allport. Ford New Zealand had decided that they could bring out a Paul Radisich signature-model road car, based on the publicity they would generate during the series.

> *I remember Garry [Jackson, from Ford New Zealand] saying that they had a heap of the base models and didn't know what to do with them.*
>
> *The standard car was like driving your lounge suite, because it wallowed all around the joint; so we stiffened it up a bit, so not only did it look good, we turned it into a little sports car. We put in a special steering wheel, up-rated the suspension, lowered it, put on new wheels, included a custom paint job and transformed it.*

Ford New Zealand intended to build 300 of the signature models, all of them in cobalt blue, but sales were so good that they eventually delivered 500. It certainly helped the marketing cause that on the track Paul won the first race, which was held at Bay Park. He and Nigel filled in their in-between race hours jet-skiing. After performing well in two more races, Paul went back to England to fulfil his other racing obligations, and Australian driver Tony Longhurst took over the seat. Nigel ended up as the meat in an accident sandwich when he collided with Brett Riley and was ignominiously T-boned by his own team-mate. He wasn't hurt, but his pride was dented almost as much as the car.

With Ford having put the Andy Rouse contract up for contention, Paul was in for a change for the 1996 British Touring

Car season. However, the team that took the contract, West Surrey Racing (WSR), did at least have a few Kiwis involved. It was part-owned by New Zealander Dick Bennetts, and was at the time a highly successful specialist single-seater team. Dick had become a recognized guru in the development of young open-wheel drivers, but by the mid-1990s he was becoming a little bored with it all. During the 1995 season he went to Brands Hatch to see a touring-car race. There, he ran into Paul, who in turn introduced him to John Griffiths of Ford Motor Company, and from that moment WSR was in the framework for the Mondeo BTCC contract.

Dick's business partner in WSR was another Auckland Westie, Mike Ewan, who was about 16 years old when he first met Paul at the local slot-car track in Henderson. He had gone to England in 1986 to work with Dick Bennetts, and had remained there ever since.

Highly successful in Formula 3 WSR might have been, but none of them had any experience with touring cars whatsoever; something that did not go unnoticed in the wider motor-sport community. Yet they were pitching to run the Mondeos in the BTCC, and pitching successfully at that. Andy Rouse Engineering lost the contract.

In fact, the last time Dick Bennetts had engineered a touring car was back in New Zealand in 1971 with Dennis Marwood and the Chev Camaro. He says now that they totally underestimated what was involved and how much it would all cost. Reynards were to build the chassis, but they didn't have a great deal of experience in this department either, having never built a front-wheel-drive car before, ever. Together, they were thrown in at the very deep end.

Andy Rouse believes WSR severely undercut him on the contract pitch, and he's right. But Peter Gillitzer's financial slash-and-burn cost-cutting regime was firmly in place, and if Ford thought WSR could do the job more cheaply, that's what they wanted.

It didn't help all of the new people involved that Ford signed off the contracts very late in the day, much like the company had done with Andy during Paul's first season. However, Dick Bennetts says that the entire blame for the poor performance of the Mondeos shouldn't lie solely with Ford. He and his partners in the venture — Reynard Special Vehicle Projects (RSVP), Cosworth, and Schuebul Engineering from Germany — were contracted to get the job done.

'That's when the fun started,' he admits, 'and we started chasing problems all year.'

Paul came with the Ford package, and his team-mate was British man Steve Robertson, whose father is now Kimi Räikkönen's manager. They managed to scrape through a media day at Donington before heading to a shake-down test at Mallory Park, but from that time forward everything began to fade, as Dick Bennetts terms it. They spent the entire season struggling to stay afloat. If you compare Paul's first season with WSR and his first season with Andy Rouse Engineering, the statistics tell the tale.

In 1993, he had three wins, two fastest laps, two pole positions, came third in the championship without contesting all events, and won the World Touring Car Cup at Monza. With WSR in 1996, he didn't have one podium finish, there were no poles, he didn't record a fastest lap, and was 13th overall in the series. He'd gone backwards.

Although there were hopes of an improvement in the second year with WSR, it wasn't much better than the first, even with a new team-mate in the shape of the fast and vastly experienced British driver Will Hoy. Dick Bennetts was concerned that the lack of money meant compromised safety, and he threatened to boycott the first race of the new season because he felt that the cars were too dangerous to drive. He had worked until 4am trying to solve a multitude of problems, and he told Ford that he wasn't prepared to put the drivers' lives at risk unnecessarily.

'I remember thinking that if this is touring cars, I'm not sure I'm enjoying it.'

Neither was Paul, and he began to question his decision to stay with Ford at a time when he'd had a number of offers to go to other teams.

> *I actually turned down Vauxhall and Volvo before I even had another deal, but I wanted to remain loyal to Ford because they had given me the opportunity to come over to Britain and show my wares. Even though money was important at that stage, loyalty to everyone was much greater. Maybe I should have jumped ship*

way before that, when I had the opportunity, but I was
always sold on 'stick with us'. Ford wanted me to stay
on and that was nice, but from my career point of view
it probably killed it.

All in all it was a disastrous couple of years for everyone involved with WSR, and at the end of that second season Paul felt he had little option but go to elsewhere, to say goodbye to the team in Shepperton that was liberally littered with expatriate Kiwis, friends for the most part, and a team that had a good engineering record in single-seaters but hadn't been able to produce the goods in touring cars.

West Surrey Racing's budget to run the Mondeo British Touring Car programme was about half what Renault was spending — and it showed. In 1996, Alain Menu won the championship in the Renault Laguna, with his team-mate Jason Plato in third. Frank Biela in the Audi A4 was sandwiched in between them. Ford didn't even make it to the top five in the manufacturers' title. Paul finished 13th and Will Hoy 15th.

Mike Ewan, a man who'd known Paul most of his life, was surprised at Paul's decision to leave, because despite the engineering issues he felt that the team was making ground and believed that they could get on top of the problems by the start of 1998. He was even more staggered that Paul chose to go to Peugeot, because their cars had suffered constantly from disintegrating engines and gearboxes, and had never had a podium finish in British Touring Cars. But Paul felt strongly that he needed a change.

Everyone said the Mondeo was the car to have and I was the quickest driver in the team, but at that point I was a driver who did not have the hardware. But I was well established in Ford and had a good relationship with everyone, and you get swept up in what is being said in meetings. If I had been really hard-nosed about it I would have looked at it in a more cynical way and realized that we weren't going to be in front. It comes back to the loyalty thing, too, and I was appreciative of Ford's commitment to me, which is great — but at the end of the day the sport is cut-throat.

He hadn't driven any type of car other than the Mondeo in the seven years he'd been in England, not even a four-cylinder car. He thinks he may have got another year's contract out of Ford, but, then again, maybe not. No one at WSR wanted him to leave, but he'd got to the point where he needed a change of scenery even if, to this day, he doesn't know whether he made the right decision or not.

So, for all these reasons, Paul changed camps to Peugeot. No, they hadn't sparkled in British Touring Cars, but with a new manager, with the right sort of funding — which they thought they were going to get — some favourable circumstances, a decent driver, and a bucketload of luck, they really thought they could improve. There was an added attraction for Paul, too. His girlfriend of the time, Patricia Watson, was working for Peugeot. Team manager Mick Linford had poached her from the John Watson Driving School at Silverstone, where she'd got a job after-event-managing a Royal gala production of the stage show *'Allo, 'Allo*. No stranger to motor sport, Patricia used to go to Silverstone with her father to watch the races. Mick regarded her job competence so highly that he talked her into managing the public relations and media role for Peugeot Motorsport. And when it came to getting Paul on the team, Mick asked her to ask Paul whether he could be lured away from Ford. She did and he could.

In the end Paul was wooed by the promise of the French Super Touring car and engine, which was a championship-winning package, along with the collaboration with Motor Sport Developments and a respected engineer.

Patricia resigned from her public relations role with the team shortly afterwards to join the BTCC radio broadcasting service, because she thought it wasn't 'politic' to work alongside Paul.

West Surrey Racing continued with the Ford programme for another year. Paul's long-time friend and contemporary from New Zealand, Craig Baird, took over at WSR where Paul had left off. Craig's team-mate for some of the season was none other than Nigel Mansell, the man Paul had teamed with a few years earlier, the famous Brit he had given pointers to about driving touring cars.

He may have been going to a new team in a new car, but Paul knew the series and the players involved and could bring that experience to any team. It was a new adventure, but also *très familier*.

Chapter 10

Bonjour, monsieur

I knew I wasn't going to be any better than where I currently was, but there was a carrot at the end of the stick.

As the 1998 season began, there were high hopes that Peugeot's fortunes in the British Touring Car Championship season might be on the rise. After all, they had decided to hire a driver at the top of his game, a double World Touring Car Cup title-holder, even if he'd had a poor couple of seasons since.

His new team-mate was Tim Harvey, whom Paul had driven with back in 1992, when they were both invited to contest a long-distance race at Brands Hatch in a Ford Sierra RS500 featuring La Batts livery. The team was owned by a well-heeled helicopter service and repairman, Lawrence Bristow. Paul's invitation to drive in this event had come on the back of his class win at the Fuji 500 in the BMW with Derek Higgins. 'Lawrence asked me how much I wanted and I said 500 quid, which he said was outrageous! So I went up there and didn't even get to drive in the end, but after a bit of pestering Lawrence paid up.'

Before the British season got underway, they took the

Peugeot 406 to Bathurst. Their team-mates in the second car were Englishman Patrick Watts, who had driven for Peugeot in Britain, and the Australian television-commentator-cum-racing-driver, Neil Crompton. The event was known as the AMP 1000 at that stage, and was the first race held there for Supertouring cars after the controversial split between the Australian Racing Drivers' Club and AVESCO (V8 Supercars).

The car qualified third on the grid but, although the Peugeot felt good, it failed to finish because of a suspension break. The British touring cars were, after all, designed primarily for sprint races, so trying to race an entire day on a mountain was asking a great deal. They jumped on a plane for the long trek back to England and looked forward to better things for the start of the new season.

Peugeot's motor-sport team in BTCC was headed by the quietly spoken and gentlemanly Mick Linford, who was head-hunted by Peugeot from the John Watson Performance Driving Centre at Silverstone. He had had some prior dealings with the French company when he encouraged the driving school to get out of the 'embarrassing' British Leyland MG Montegos they were using at the race school, and the equally embarrassing Maestros they were employing for the rally school, and switch to Peugeots.

In 1995, Mick was asked to head Peugeot Motorsport. In fact, the first approach was so casual that he took it for a throwaway line and didn't follow through, and it was only when they telephoned him and asked him specifically about the role that he realized they were serious.

It is fair to say that the French marque hadn't had a lot of success in British Touring Cars, and Peugeot Motorsport UK certainly lacked the funding of some of the other European teams. When they first began in the competition in 1995, they'd haul the race car on the back of a trailer. Everyone else (or the works teams at least) would use transporters, so by comparison Peugeot's efforts looked like they were turning up for a club meeting. One of the first jobs on Mick's list was to buy the team a transporter. Even when they did get hold of one, it wasn't a state-of-the-art transporter as enjoyed by the likes of the BMW or Alfa Romeo teams; it was second-hand, and highlighted the budget constraints they faced.

Mick Linford had decided that rather than try to manage the performance engines in-house for what was essentially a minor brand in the UK, he would farm out the job to Motor Sport Developments (MSD). It would cost more, but the plan was to bring MSD's experience and knowledge to the Peugeot framework, because they genuinely wanted to stride forward in the championship. David Whitehead and his team at MSD had been managing Honda's engines in BTCC and had engineered the Hyundai World Rally Championship engines before that.

Also in their employ was the highly respected and vastly experienced engineer Eddie Hinckley, whose curriculum vitae included working on the Jaguar World Sportscar Championship (with a 1988 Le Mans win). He had worked with Alfa Romeo in German Touring Cars, and was race engineer on David Leslie's Honda in British Touring Cars before being enticed to Peugeot.

Tim Harvey was a well-established and competent driver. His former team-mates included Alain Menu, Steve Soper, Rickard Rydell, and Andy Rouse. Paul replaced Patrick Watts. All in all, the calibre of the personnel in the new team Paul signed with was unquestioned. What was needed, as Paul freely acknowledges, was for the cars to come up to speed.

As can happen in motor racing, Peugeot made promises, including that they would pick up the French programme and that I would become aligned with that.

We thought we would work on one year of hell and that would turn into one year with a competitive package, so I weighed all that up and made the decision to jump into the Peugeot.

Like Paul, Tim Harvey had started his racing career in motocross, an uncommon path to take; unlike Paul, he then continued through the more traditional ranks of karts and Formula Ford, before climbing into a British Touring Car. He's not sure he'd agree with Frank Radisich that motocross grants the ability to set a quick time on a new circuit, but they're like-minded that the feel and balance required for bikes is a handy ability for car racing, particularly in wet-weather racing.

Some serious rule changes were introduced for the 1998 season, more so than at any other time in the championship's 40-year history. Some of the technical changes were supposed to save money and to slow the cars down, but format changes were also introduced. Each round would now include two races: a short sprint race and a longer feature race. The sprint race was non-stop, while the feature race was double the number of laps of the sprint race and included a compulsory pit stop to change at least two tyres. Qualifying included a one-shot showdown, where drivers had just one flying lap for a qualifying time, remarkably like the V8 Supercars top 10 shoot-out, which is probably no mere coincidence.

The Peugeot 407s sported Esso Ultron sponsorship, and were dressed accordingly in green and gold as Paul arrived at the first test session at Silverstone.

> *I had tested the car at the end of the previous year and it was quick, it felt really good. It was definitely lighter up the front compared with the Mondeo, so although it felt similar in some respects, it was more nimble because it had less weight over the front, which made it more agile and easier on the tyres.*

During all the times Peugeot had been manfully contesting BTCC, the UK company had received no help at all from France. The French team were running Laurent Aiello in the German Touring Car Championship, and had initially indicated to Peugeot Motorsport UK that there would be a transfer of information. They'd indicated as much to Paul when he signed with the team, and the promise of this French assistance was certainly an inducement for him to move.

It didn't happen. Moreover, the UK Peugeot team sometimes

felt hindered by the parent company. When the British team sent one of their engines to France for a dynometer test, they wondered if the French racing technicians had tested their own engines (which were to be used as a benchmark) under far more favourable conditions than those used for the test of the UK engines. After all, these things can be done subtly.

MSD managed to extract a little more brake horsepower for the drivers during the season, even without assistance from the French, but both drivers were still constantly in the middle of the field. Neither Tim nor Paul could ever seem to break through into the top 10, and there were many heated discussions between Mick Linford and the rest of the Peugeot team and MSD about the reasons why.

It's fair to say, too, that the relationship between Tim and Paul was never entirely comfortable. There wasn't any downright open disagreement, but small niggles surfaced from time to time, and in recent times Tim has stated that he thought Paul was self-interested.

'He wasn't the best team-mate,' he says. 'Although we had always been friends, professionally as a team-mate Paul was very selfish; he did not like it when I beat him, and would go out of his way to try to get the best of everything. He did not share data well, he wouldn't want to tell me the truth. He wasn't open.'

Tim said this with a grin on his face, something he wears often. It may account for his nickname around the pits of the 'Smiling Assassin', and his viewpoint wasn't always shared by others in the team. Certainly Mick Linford snorted when he heard what Tim had said; he considers Paul's approach entirely normal.

If Paul had asked his engineer not to pass information on until it could be proven, Mick said, that was normal and such data would eventually be shared under normal team protocol. Indeed, throughout what turned out to be a very frustrating year for both drivers, Mark never once saw Paul lose his cool or blame everyone else for his woes. The best he could muster was annoyance at the car's non-performance, which hardly threatened team unity because they all felt the same way. He thinks Paul was always utterly professional and generated good team spirit.

If he had an ego he kept it completely under control. He had reached the ultimate in his field, and he was only interested in results, whereas other drivers could throw their toys out of the pram.

At the start of the season, Tim made it clear he needed certain things to retain an image. He was offered a 'milky yellow' Peugeot 406 coupé as his personal drive car, but turned it down, saying it was far too much of a 'girl's colour'.

Paul says that he and Tim would talk together within the team structure and at the race track, and occasionally they would socialize, but if they didn't have any major verbal stoushes, neither were they close.

'Tim had been there for a while and was well established, so he was trying to work things around for himself and I was the new guy coming in and trying to get settled. The first year was going to be the hardest, and if we'd had two years together I could have probably had a good relationship with him, but I felt

149

you could never fully trust him, so I never opened out that much. It certainly didn't help that the equipment wasn't that good, and we were both frustrated in that department.'

The best result all season was Tim's excellent second to Gabriele Tarquini in the Alfa Romeo at Thruxton, which Tim says Paul was 'miffed' about. It's tempting to say that, as a serious and highly competitive racing driver, why would Paul not be? He always wanted to win.

Tim considered Paul would 'rag' the cars, that he was hard on the tyres and chassis, but Mick Linford says Paul drove as hard and as fast as he could, and besides, he wasn't nearly as firm on gears as Patrick Watts had been, the man who was known to annihilate ratios quicker than punk bands trash guitars.

At the end of the 1998 season, Paul was 14th in the championship and Tim Harvey was 17th — so much for Paul being miffed about being beaten. However, even if the Peugeot team had shown tantalizing potential with Tim's podium finish, it seemed that no matter what the drivers, engineers and management did it wasn't enough. It became disheartening, and in the meantime other teams that had healthy budgets were forging ahead in terms of development and results.

Some of these difficulties began to manifest in other ways, and at times Mick Linford felt under siege. He thought that Alan Gow, the boss of the British Touring Car Series and a personal friend of Paul's, was more 'obliging' to the bigger teams with larger budgets. Whether that's true or not, Peugeot could only look in wonderment at what some of the wealthier teams were spending. The frontrunners wouldn't have had any change from £5 million per car. Others might say that they were 'only' spending £3 million, but a closer examination of the books might reveal many more costs hidden under different headings. For a team like Vauxhall to say that they were only spending £4 million was, according to Mick Linford, crap.

The drivers, too, could only look in wonderment at the salaries of some other competitors. Alain Menu was reportedly on £600,000 a year. Paul was receiving about what he'd been paid at WSR, because Peugeot knew that they had to match his existing salary. But a driver needs to be winning in order to capitalize on personal marketing opportunities — and Paul wasn't winning.

The problems simmering within the Peugeot team became more overt towards the end of 1997 and going into the 1998 season. Motor Sport Developments (MSD) was in turmoil, with staff chopping and changing. Eddie Hinckley, one of the inducements used as a carrot to get Paul to sign the Peugeot contract, resigned to go to Audisport UK, and along with him went a considerable amount of specialist knowledge. The number of new faces in the team didn't help with continuity, and Paul felt as if no one was able to get on top of these things with sufficient urgency.

I had to start rebuilding again in many ways. They had modified the car slightly, but there were engineering issues with the back of the car — design faults — which were causing some worry.

Peugeot car dealers were also asking why Peugeot couldn't get further up the grid. They would journey to the races, enjoy the conviviality of fellow dealers and other guests, sponsors, and marketing people, imbibe a decent white or a saucy little red (French probably) and dine well. It was a great day out. Except, they weren't winning.

The bottom line was that the race team lacked enough money to get on the podium, even if those in the hospitality suite thought they were spending sufficient amounts. Car dealers are the first to query any deal not of their own making. They knew that on Monday morning they might find their lack of results hard to explain to a prospective customer, and that, in the end, was what racing in this series was all about.

One thing was certain: Paul knew he didn't want to spend another season at this level. He had won two World Touring Car titles with Andy Rouse only to labour with Ford and West Surrey Racing for two seasons, and here he was doing it all again, failing to make an impression. Like the rest of the team, he was feeling very perturbed indeed. If there was some consolation, it lay in the fact he was about equal with the Ford Mondeos.

I didn't go forwards and I didn't go backwards either, because I couldn't go any further backwards!

Peugeot pulled the pin on their BTCC programme towards the end of 1998, by which time all of the other potential seats in

BTCC were already taken. There wasn't anywhere else for Paul to go — if he wanted to continue driving, he knew he had to consider his options outside the UK. He wasn't looking for a change of career, but he had to ponder a change of place and leave behind the life he had led for the past eight years.

As a corollary to the Peugeot story, the team reappeared in BTCC in 2001 and talked the legendary Steve Soper into coming out of semi-retirement to partner Matt Neal, who had dominated the independent category in 2000, and the rookie Dan Eaves. Soper was one of Paul's old adversaries. He had been synonymous with BMW success in Europe, in BTCC, in the Wellington street race, and at Bathurst. He was 48 years old.

Mick Linford retired from the sport, and Vic Lee took over as the new team boss. Further rule changes that had been brought in for that season with the aim of reducing costs certainly helped Peugeot. Dan Eaves came fifth, Steve Soper sixth and Matt Neal 14th. The company withdrew from the championship again at the end of the 2001 season to concentrate on rallying, recruiting Richard Burns to spearhead the attack.

In the meantime, Paul decided to come home, or at least as near to home as he had been for years. His destination: Australia. The competition: V8 Supercars.

Chapter 11

The tribal council has spoken

Being in Australia was like being on holiday after eight years of cold English weather.

In 1999, when Paul made his debut in the Australian touring-car series, he found that he was entering a series that was held in considerable esteem by the public. Two years earlier, the marketing and promotion of touring-car racing in Australia had been wrested from the governing body, the Confederation of Australian Motor Sport (CAMS), by sports marketing company IMG after a fairly acrimonious battle between CAMS and the Australian Racing Drivers' Club (ARDC), which ran and promoted a couple of events, including the jewel in the crown, Bathurst. The ARDC had introduced the glamour event, the Bathurst 1000, to Mt Panorama. In fact, the head of ARDC, Ivan Stibbard, was known as 'Mr Bathurst', so to lose the event must have been a bitter pill to swallow.

IMG changed the name of the series to V8 Supercars and hooked in Network Ten to replace Channel Seven, all of which resulted in a huge increase of interest in the sport from sponsors, advertisers and (most importantly) fans. It's an example of what the Wellington street-race promoter, Ian Gamble, would often cite: the successful promotion of any sport should not be in the hands of the governing body. He used to say that if one needed to form a committee of three to put on an event, any event, it was best if the other two didn't turn up.

The Australian Vee Eight Supercar Company (AVESCO) was later formed to run the series directly, and became independent from its IMG origins. The name was changed to V8 Supercars Australia in 2005.

The year before Paul joined the series, one of its high-profile drivers was contemplating his retirement from the team with which he had had a long and successful association. Tasmanian driver John Bowe had decided to move from Dick Johnson Racing to the Caterpillar team, but before the season was out that team was sold to Queensland car dealer John Briggs.

Also retiring in 1997 — but for good, not just from his team — was Peter Brock. Paul had had the advantage of having worked with both Brock and Dick Johnson, and with that personal connection came the possibility of a seat on either team. Adding to his attractiveness as a driver was his years of racing in the UK, and his two World Touring Car Cup titles.

However, Peter Brock's place had been taken by Mark Skaife. The former Nissan works driver was an ideal Australian candidate for the iconic Holden Racing Team to partner the young and very talented Craig Lowndes, who had joined the team the season before, in 1996. So, as far as Paul was concerned, two of the potentially best driving seats in Australian V8 Supercars were already filled. That left Dick Johnson Racing, which towards the end of 1997 still had a vacancy. Dick had never hired a New Zealander as a full-time driver before, but he certainly had plenty of them in his team, on the mechanical side of things. Indeed, at one stage almost half of Dick Johnson Racing was populated by Kiwis.

Given the public profile of V8 Supercars (which seemed to grow equally as the popularity of British Touring Cars diminished), given that Paul wasn't exactly enjoying unprecedented racing success with Peugeot in the BTCC, given that Australia is not a difficult country in which to live and work, and given Paul's former track record, there didn't need to be a lot of protracted contemplation. Besides, it would be summer in Australia, and for Paul, facing another English winter in his home in Leamington Spa, a trip south began to look very attractive.

He contacted Dick Johnson Racing's general manager, Wayne Cattach (later to become CEO of V8 Supercars), for a chat. Would he, asked Wayne, consider popping over to Australia for a meaningful discussion? Would he indeed. He was coming back to New Zealand for Christmas anyway, and it was no problem to call in on his way.

In the back of my mind I thought that after I'd finished racing in Europe I'd look at Australia. It took a bit of going backwards and forwards, and there were a few issues to be sorted through with a brand-new car, the AU Falcon.

He was offered the job for a year, so flew back to England and put the house on the market. He and Patricia were saying goodbye to eight years of their lives; some very successful years on the track, and some struggling recent years. They were leaving behind the very good friends they had made during that time, bidding farewell to a lifestyle that they had grown to love, to a social milieu within the BTCC ranks that they knew deep down would never be repeated, and they were saying goodbye to Patricia's family.

In retrospect, the remarkably truncated timeframe was a blessing in disguise, because there was little or no opportunity for anyone, let alone themselves, to lament their departure at length. Besides, because the DJR contract was only for one year, they fully expected to do the business in Australia and then come back to the UK to what they imagined would be a reinvigorated British Touring Car Championship. Little did anyone know that they were about to spend as long in Australia as they had in England.

Paul had to come to grips with a new car and a vastly different racing package than he had been used to with the front-wheel-drive 2.0-litre cars, which were nimble but which required a lot of work on the part of the driver to get lap times down. Now he had some horses under the bonnet.

For sheer thrill, the V8 was very exciting. It's a big thing and the car would wallow around and bounce and

jump all over the place, but the horsepower available
made for a very nice change.

There was also the heat to contend with. In Australia, at some tracks a sunny day can generate an in-car temperature of up to 60°C and, although he'd always been fit, Paul found he had to concentrate on a different type of fitness after coming from the colder northern climate. He had to increase his stamina to prepare for long-distance events like Sandown and Bathurst. The British Touring Car Championship had nothing similar, as it consisted entirely of sprint races.

Although Paul knew Dick Johnson from years back, accepting a drive for a one-off event is very different to being a permanent team member. Dick comes across in the media as an archetypal laid-back Aussie, the master of often very funny throwaway one-liners when he's confronted with a microphone. But as all of his drivers find out, he can also be intense, and he is passionate about his sport and his team. Dick and John Bowe's relationship had foundered towards the end of Bowe's tenure with the team, but for Paul this was a new opportunity in a new country, and in the beginning he and Dick got on well. Dick was in his retirement year and had dozens of commitments to honour outside the car. Paul's job was to literally get up to speed in the new car. 'We had an established relationship so we knew each other reasonably well and he accepted me in the team, a bit like a son in a way, so the first year was pretty good.'

Paul ripped into the Gold Coast lifestyle. He and Patricia based themselves at Sovereign Island, and he bought all the beach-side toys, including a jet-ski and a boat. One of his first outings in the boat was to Dick and Jill Johnson's favourite mooring spot on the Gold Coast, Broadwater, for some serious instruction in nautical capability.

I had just taken delivery of the new Mustang 32-footer and I managed to find Dick's boat, which was moored up on the beach with another large boat beside it. I had never tried to moor beside another boat in my life. The wind was blowing and the current was flowing fast, and by this time I was being carried along totally out of control.

I thought, 'If in doubt, power out', but I hadn't had any lessons at this point and it was the wrong thing to do — and I rammed my boat into the side of the bow on Dick's boat.

The only fortunate thing was that Dick's boat was stationary, because otherwise the damage would have been severe. Dick was gracious enough not to say too much, and they actually laughed about it, a bit later.

There were other lessons to be learned in Australia, too. During one of their first trips to Melbourne, Paul and Patricia had planned to go to dinner with Dick, Jill and their son, Steven. It was raining heavily, and at a roundabout junction their road Falcon was sideswiped by another car and shoved towards a lamppost.

I threw my arm across Patsy to save her from the

possible impact and brought the car to a stop on the footpath. The people in the other car came flying out, yelling their heads off.

I got out and the next thing I knew the driver punched me full in the face, splitting my lip. Blood was pouring everywhere, and Patsy was standing between two Greek guys and me to stop them throwing any more punches.

Just after that, Dick called to ask where we had got to and Patsy told him he'd better come back. You should have seen the other driver's face when he realized who he was confronted by. He made a hasty back-pedal and said he would never have hit me if he'd known who I was.

Steven phoned his lawyer in Queensland, who called the Melbourne police. When the police turned up they calmed the situation down and, after a bit of discussion, no charges were laid. The Ford loan car, however, was written off and had to be towed back to Moonee Ponds, the spiritual home of Dame Edna Everidge. The following day at Calder Park, Paul had trouble sliding his helmet over his fat lip, but even so he came third in the round, and no one at the post-race media conference even asked him why he'd changed his appearance.

It was one more induction ceremony into the Aussie way of life for Patricia, who still had to be totally convinced she could fall in love with the place. The huge Huntsman spiders, the cane toads and the snakes didn't help matters, and she felt like a fish out of water, to continue the critter metaphor, for the first few months. But she slowly adapted, even if she missed London and the way it was possible to indulge in spontaneous trips to mainland Europe from there.

Dick enjoys a hearty relationship with the Australian media (who are a hard bunch to please), and Paul has a similar well-founded reputation with the New Zealand media. He and Dick, then, were a good public relations combination. Dick says that, without doubt, Paul was always very good with words and he could market himself very well.

It was during his first year with Dick Johnson Racing that Paul acquired the moniker 'The Rat'. Australia is, after all, a country where abbreviating a name and sticking a suffix on the end is *de rigueur*, as evidenced by Brocky, Dicko, Steve-o and thousands of other examples. But Radisich is almost impossible to manipulate unless done subtly, which it was in New Zealand. Before he went to live in England, Paul was known around the paddock in his own country as 'Patch', thanks to the equation Radisich to radish, radish to patch. But that might have been too tame for the Australians, even if they knew 'Patch' existed at all.

There are a number of suggestions as to where and when The Rat originated. Alan Gow thought it started in England, where someone thought Paul was 'rat-like'. Another theory is that it came from the big man with an even larger voice, television commentator Darryl Eastlake. The story goes that he referred to

Paul driving 'like a rat up the rafters'. He might have done so, but that's not where The Rat emerged.

It came from a concerted marketing exercise that followed on from a suggestion from Paul Gover, the motoring and motor-sport journalist from the *Herald Sun* newspaper in Melbourne. He mentioned The Rat notion to the public relations man for Dick Johnson Racing, David Segal, but initially the concept was shelved. However, Paul thinks the idea was market-tested on a few people anyway, because it was resurrected, and has stuck ever since. It has become catchy enough to be quantified and measured in marketing terms.

The Rat merchandise eventually formed a healthy part of all of the merchandise sold from Dick Johnson Racing. The name became very familiar in New Zealand, thanks to the television coverage that comes complete with Australian commentary and the running of a round in New Zealand each year.

Paul was under contract for one season only at this stage and wasn't expected to fly out of the box. It was really a chance for him to get to know the tracks. The car wasn't always competitive, either, and he eventually finished in 16th place in the championship. Dick, driving in his final year, came 10th, and was replaced by his son Steven. Paul acted as his mentor in the beginning, and there was a great deal of expectation from the family, and to a certain extent from the wider public, for Steven to prove himself as Dick's successor.

In 2000, Paul's results began to consolidate and he recorded his first win, at Sandown. He followed that up with a win in the next round at the Surfer's Paradise IndyCar event, and eventually finished fourth in the series behind Mark Skaife, Garth Tander and Craig Lowndes. Strewth, he deserved a Fosters, but!

To all intents and purposes, it looked as though it was going to get even better the following year, but as the 2001 season progressed the results weren't quite as they'd hoped. Overall it wasn't too bad, though. Paul finished seventh in the series and prepared to start yet another year with Dick Johnson Racing.

Steven and Paul did have at least one thing in common: both of them worked closely with their fathers in their motor-sport career. When he was starting out in the sport, Paul had made a conscious decision to refer to his father by his name, Frank, rather than calling him 'Dad'. At home, he'll call him 'Dad'; in public, he's 'Frank'. It arose out of a personal horror he had of calling out 'Daaaad' in the pits like a three-year-old; it wasn't quite the image he wanted to present as a professional driver. Steven, on the other hand, has no such qualms.

At the end of the season Paul's contract with the team was extended for a further three years, but not without some difficulty. More parties became involved in his contractual arrangement, and it was no longer simply an agreement between him and Dick Johnson. It now included Ford Motor Company and Shell.

Ford wanted me to stay with DJR; Shell wanted me to stay, too. So Dick was sort of pressured into taking me, but I don't think he particularly wanted me to stay. I think in his mind he had his arm forced up his back, and from there on our relationship began to sour. Dick doesn't particularly like being told what to do.

As Steven began to improve his placings, to get up to speed on the race track, he no longer needed quite the mentoring from Paul that he had previously received. He now viewed Paul — probably rightly if one is to be competitive — as opposition, even if they were in the same team. For Paul there was also the added difficulty of dealing with the family firm. He was working with a tribal council of Johnsons, and the axiom that blood is thicker than water applied. Anyone not part of the family set-up felt the natural phenomenon of being an 'outsider', however slight it might be. It was somewhat like being married but never being fully accepted by the in-laws.

It didn't help that the development programme on the AU stagnated; they weren't making the ground they wanted to, and Paul had to retire three times from races over the season, which didn't improve the team's position on the points table. From about that period, the arguments between the Johnsons and Paul increased and the relationship degenerated. In Paul's mind, the biggest issue between them stemmed from the contract.

Dick had been forced by Ford and Shell to take me on. Maybe I was getting more than Dick and he felt he shouldn't be paying a driver that amount of money, particularly since I didn't have the responsibility of running the team.

Paul's best placing was fourth in the final round, but he finished well down the pack at the end of the series and he was miserable. There was never any suggestion that Paul was given inferior equipment, as can happen in some teams. His concerns centred on people management. His talent remained obvious — sufficient for journalist Andrew McLean to describe him at this time in typical Australian jargonese: 'as cunning as his [Rat] nickname suggests, as hard to pass as a kidney stone and as fast as a Jimi Hendrix guitar solo'.

Whatever the reasons, and they are many and varied, Dick Johnson decided to relinquish Paul's services. The feeling was mutual, because the atmosphere had been uncomfortable for quite some time. The official line was that Paul wasn't 'integrating' in the team. 'This was such an important element in the success of the team,' said Dick Johnson, 'that we decided it was best to part ways.'

It wasn't quite that straightforward, however. Paul was in England at that time, and he had a contract firmly in place. Dick had to do something he didn't want to, which was to buy him out. But he was a man of his word and he honoured the contract, and — as Paul was to find out — there are others in the racing business who don't have the same honesty and integrity. Paul had given DJR four seasons, but he had to look elsewhere for his future employment.

Since then, DJR appears to have had as many drivers (apart from

Dick's son Steven) as Budget Cabs on a 24-hour shift. They include Max Wilson, Warren Luff, Glenn Seton and Will Davison.

DJR is the oldest team in the V8 Supercar franchise. Since around 2001 they've struggled to consistently stay at the top, and financially it has certainly been a worry, even if Dick Johnson has orchestrated some entrepreneurial sponsorship.

His very long and successful association with Shell Helix ended in 2002, shortly after Dick retired from active driving. In 2005, in an association with Warner Brothers, the team introduced characters from the *Wacky Races* cartoon series, like Dick Dastardly, Muttley and Penelope Pitstop. They and the Flintstones appeared on DJR cars and merchandise, and, in a motor-sport world populated by shallow press releases, the one announcing this tie-in was a classic example of triteness. It quoted Dick Johnson as saying the Flintstones are a family like the Johnsons, and gave rise to a few in the media room referring to Steven as 'Bam Bam'. But only out of earshot, of course.

Dick formed a company called First Rock Mortgages, so named after his famous Bathurst race of 1980 when his car struck a rock and rolled down the bank, and at the same time he put his name to the marketing of 'V8' telephones via Telecom. In 2006, he acquired whiskey manufacturer Jim Beam as naming-rights sponsor, thus assuring his son and co-driver Will Davison of their racing seats.

The Westpoint Group had filled the financial void left when Shell withdrew its sponsorship, but that company's spectacular A$300 million collapse in 2005 left substantial unpaid sponsorship bills and a stock of useless merchandise. Dick's companies couldn't fill the financial shortfall: DJR was in trouble. One of Australia's highest-profile racing drivers and team owners, Dick threatened to walk away from the sport altogether.

In February 2008, Dick Johnson formed a partnership arrangement with Australian 'Forklift King' Charlie Schwerkolt, whose only association with V8 Supercars before this had been as a supplier of forklifts for recovery work, and as the forklift supplier for building the Melbourne Grand Prix and Gold Coast Indy circuits. For Dick Johnson and the family, it meant a significant restructure, but it also meant that DJR was out of the financial mire.

These events show the sometimes precarious nature of V8 Supercars, and illustrate how expensive it is, both as a sport and a business. What they don't show, as with any business, are the manifold workings that go on behind the public façade, which can affect different people in a variety of ways.

Paul understands this as much as anybody, and when the decision to leave DJR was made, he was heading for a brand new team, but he wasn't leaping into the unknown. He believed his opportunities for team involvement and the all-important podium finishes would improve, but no one — himself, Patricia, his family back in New Zealand, or indeed his supporters — could know that this would be the calm before the storm.

The tempest in this case came in the guise of the man who headed the Triple Eight Racing team, a man who, according to some who have had dealings with him both in the UK and Australia, is best treated with circumspection.

Chapter 12

It's all true — and it's totally false

I was astonished. Obviously we had a major disagreement of the highest level.

In 2003, five years after Paul Radisich had moved from the UK to Australia, and after five hectic years of racing in the V8 Supercar series, he realized there was to be a parting of the ways with Dick Johnson Racing. The decision had been forced upon him in many ways, and, as is usual in motor racing, the next step was crucial.

In the 'silly season' of driver departures and new hirings, the doors to any and every team are not exactly wide open. By the end of a season, team managers have generally been talking to drivers about a potential change for some six months, if not longer. Paul had an advantage during this phase, as he at least knew a few people in the scene. Indeed, he was approached by an Englishman who was keen for him to open the door so that he could begin negotiations to purchase a team.

Paul obliged, and so introduced Triple Eight Racing to V8 Supercars in Australia.

The team was originally formed in the UK in 1996 to design,

build and race a Super Touring Vectra Coupé on behalf of Vauxhall Motors in the British Touring Car Championship. The car gave Triple Eight unprecedented success by winning the manufacturer's, driver's and team's titles four years running, although, it has to be said, this was at a time when there were far fewer manufacturers involved in BTCC than in the days when Paul had been involved in the competition. Still, Triple Eight had an impressive record.

There were four team owners, including Roland Dane, who reportedly made as much as £20 million during his time as a car dealer in the UK. He was a witness in a British Ministry of Trade and Industry Select Committee hearing on parallel importing in 1999, representing the British Independent Motor Trade Association, so he does have some horsepower when it comes to vehicles and the selling thereof.

Dane was joined by his BTCC business partner and friend, Irishman Peter Butterly, who hails from the small seaside town of Rush, about 25 kilometres from Dublin. He owned the largest car distribution operation in Europe for many years, and through it he met Roland Dane. He has property interests in Ireland and South Australia, and owns a couple of houses: one in Surfer's Paradise; and the other in Port Hughes, a small coastal town on the Cooper Coast of South Australia, on the Northern Yorke Peninsula. Around the team he is known simply as 'PB', as was Peter Brock.

Derek Warwick has the highest public profile of the four Triple Eight owners. He won the British Formula 3 championship in 1978, and went on to compete in 147 Formula 1 Grands Prix, never winning a race but gaining 71 points during his career.

During the early part of the 1980s he was thought more likely to win the World Formula 1 driver's title than Nigel Mansell, but career choices stymied his progress. Before switching to British Touring Cars, he won the World Sportscar Championship in 1992, and in the same year was part of the Peugeot team that won the 24 Hours of Le Mans. He has also raced Grand Prix Masters and owns a couple of car dealerships.

Englishman Ian Harrison runs Triple Eight in the UK. He has spent over 33 years in motor racing, working on a variety of exotic cars for high-profile teams. He is a former Williams Renault Formula 1 team manager, and was team manager for Silk Cut Jaguar in World Sports Prototypes until he joined Triple Eight to contest British Touring Cars. In his spare time, he sails the North Atlantic or the Irish Sea, which takes courage at the best of times.

In 2002, Roland Dane and Derek Warwick sold their interest in Triple Eight (UK) to Ian Harrison, thus essentially quitting the British Touring Cars Championship to make way for their new venture Down Under. Collectively, the knowledge and experience this quartet could bring to Australian V8 Supercars was vast. There was certainly an opening for this highly successful team to expand their operations into Australia: all it took was an interest (which they certainly had), some expertise (they had that too), hiring some local staff and, of course, money.

Paul knew that Roland Dane and his partners had been trying to buy into the Holden Dealer Team, but weren't making any progress. As he describes it, they were sniffing around the V8 paddock, and Roland had telephoned him a couple of times. He mentioned to John Briggs that his acquaintances from England, a couple of men he considered to be friends, were interested in entering Australian V8 Supercars as owners. John asked him to initiate discussions and Paul went back to Roland Dane.

At the time, Briggs Motorsport was owned by Brisbane car dealer, John Briggs. Max Wilson and Tony Longhurst drove for the team in 2002. Paul joined them in the following year, when the team was known to be open to an offer. Paul considered that John Briggs ran a tight little ship: they were regularly mid-field, in and around the top 15, but on occasion they were more competitive. Paul had enjoyed his time there.

The upshot of the discussions between Roland Dane, Paul Radisich and John Briggs was that Triple Eight purchased the John Briggs Motorsport V8 franchise, so acquiring all the paraphernalia, including the racing Falcon. In effect, Paul brokered the deal. The team principals were, after all, setting up business in Australia for the first time in their lives. For his efforts in helping them do so, the agreement was that Paul would not only drive for the team, but would acquire shares in the team.

The plan along the way was to do a couple of years of racing and then perhaps become involved in the team side of things, and I was very comfortable with that. I knew that Roland was extremely well organized and a very sharp businessman, and that he would definitely be able to take it to the next level.

It all looked very good, and when they took over the team I had a contract with John Briggs as a driver for one year. Because I was involved with the English guys I felt there was no need to raise the issue about contracts, because my contract with Briggs came with the purchase of the company.

Triple Eight also took over the Betta Electrical sponsorship from Briggs Motorsport. As a driver, of course, Paul had had a relationship with the company when the team was owned by John Briggs, and he endorsed Roland Dane to the sponsor because, as he says, Betta Electrical did not know who Dane was.

One of the major investors in the acquisition of the Briggs team was Ford Australia, and with this sort of backing the Triple Eight team set up shop at a new and custom-built base at Bowen Hills, a suburb of Brisbane. They initially employed over 35 people, among whom was New Zealander Campbell Little, the tall man with a short surname who was 'enticed' from Stone Brothers Racing. He is considered a very astute and capable race engineer and is highly regarded by colleagues and competitors alike — not a common thing in an arena that frequently suffers from ego overload. Importantly, he brought with him insider knowledge of the operations of a competitor. Other engineering decisions were discussed with the UK-based operation, and the new owners brought in some staff from the UK. Principal among these was the French technical director, Ludovic Lacroix.

At the time, Paul's friend and mentor Alan Gow, who had had some experience dealing with Roland Dane in British Touring Cars, expressed reservations at Paul joining Triple Eight:

In my opinion, Roland is a thoroughly dislikeable person, and when Paul said he was going to drive for his team I told him to be very careful of Dane, because it wouldn't last.

Yet despite these words of caution and the misgivings of a number of other people, Paul thought that team unity and a gentleman's agreement would be of paramount importance; after all, he was brokering the deal for and on behalf of the team. He decided to venture forward; he would be intricately involved, more so than as 'just' a driver. In reality there were not a lot of driving options open to him, but neither had they disappeared altogether. He wanted the dual role of racer and businessman.

No one expected Paul to be up at the front in the first season (2003), but he finished 10th in the series, which showed he was, as he says, 'steaming along' quite nicely. He was partnered in the long-distance events by the Australian, Dean Canto. The following year, Max Wilson left Dick Johnson Racing after one season and joined Triple Eight in a two-car team.

Although his name sounds frightfully English, Max Wilson is actually Brazilian. He has a similar career path to Paul, inasmuch as they had both tried to make it into Formula 1. In fact, Max had been a test driver for Williams in 1998 and was once offered a position with Minardi, but turned it down. He tried to establish a consistent Champcar drive in the USA but, as is so often the case, the money just wasn't there. He heard about V8 Supercars from some friends, headed to Australia, settled on the Gold Coast and was hired by Briggs Motorsport.

Paul enjoyed a good relationship with the South American, who is probably the smallest of all the current V8 Supercar drivers and could pass for a jockey. He says Max was always happy and a nice guy to have around. Whenever they finished a race, Max would always congratulate him, and not, says Paul, through gritted teeth like some team-mates he'd had in the past. Max, as it happens, is on Paul's list of team-mates that he has most admired over the years, along with Nigel Mansell and Jeff Allam.

Triple Eight fortuitously managed to acquire appropriate race numbers for their cars by taking 888 from the Ozemail team of Brad Jones and giving it to Max Wilson; this would avoid any confusion by the commentators and others with Paul's BA Falcon which was running with 88. In hindsight it's tempting to say that with that number on the side of his car, Paul ended up one digit short of a full hand, but back then he didn't know what would unfold in the future.

For all of the second season, Betta Electrical Falcons failed to make any sort of significant contribution to the time-sheets. No matter how much engineering expertise a team has, building two new cars and developing a brand-new team from scratch and getting to the front end of the field in the first season is not just a formidable task, it's well-nigh impossible. In the second season, though, people are expected to produce results. But both Triple Eight cars were dogged by mechanical problems of varying sorts.

There were times when the sheer speed of both cars was up to front-runner standards, but mechanical gremlins kept getting in the way and couldn't, apparently, be rectified. Come Bathurst time, there were serious concerns about the engineering of the cars, and, as a consequence, the safety aspects. Things had a habit of breaking or falling off, and both drivers knew that the uprights on the car simply weren't strong enough. Max broke one in practice and was lucky not to hit the wall.

Paul also broke an upright, and it probably didn't help matters that when this happened Patricia phoned Peter Butterly and vented her spleen at what she saw as potentially fatal consequences. She knew enough to know that it wasn't safe, and said so. Many a man working in this environment wouldn't take kindly to a woman, even one as attractive as Patricia, ticking them off, but the end-of-year results were telling. Paul was 19th and Max a lowly 28th.

Still, there were hopes they could mould the team, improve on the cars and move up the time-sheets, and at season's end this was what Paul was expecting. He had done the hard yards with the car and he was the higher placed of the two drivers. Then the telephone rang.

Paul had had such significant telephone conversations before and they had often turned out well, but he never, ever, expected to receive one like this. Roland Dane immediately started to say 'ah' and 'um' and, cough, cough, 'hello'. He couldn't seem to get out what he wanted to say. Something was clearly catching in his throat and, as it turned out, it was something that Paul didn't want to hear.

He finally came out and said that I would be replaced in August. I was totally dumbfounded and I don't think I said anything in reply. That's when he told me that Craig Lowndes was coming in and that, since Max was under contract to the team and I wasn't, he had to let me go.

Paul was, not unexpectedly, perturbed, angry and confused, and went to see Roland Dane. It was then that he found out that the Lowndes deal was done, it was a *fait accompli*, and Paul's contract was not up for negotiation. He sought permission to see Peter Butterly at his home on the Gold Coast, because clearly Paul needed to talk further. Butterly suggested that under the circumstances the relationship had broken down, and that he felt it would be better for all parties involved if Paul packed his bags and left the team immediately. It was a situation created by the team, yet essentially here was one of the principals blaming and punishing Paul for his consequent frustration.

Craig Lowndes was considered the golden boy of Australian motor racing. He'd had considerable success with the iconic Holden Racing Team in V8 Supercars before being poached by and contracted to Ford. He completed four years with Ford Performance Racing (or Tickford Engineering as it was then), but mechanical problems hadn't allowed him to show his strengths. Nevertheless, remarkably he was still one of the highest-profile drivers in the series.

Ford decided to relinquish its sponsorship of the Australian Tennis Open (estimated to be worth between $10 million and

$12 million) and to spread that money amongst all of the Ford teams in V8 Supercars. They wanted — in fact, needed — to have a higher podium presence in the series and not be consistently beaten by Holden. Roland Dane seems to have convinced Ford that he would be able to get the personable Lowndes back on the podium in a competitive car, which was ambitious at least and astonishing at worst, given the team's record that season. But Lowndes fitted Ford's criteria, and from a purely commercial standpoint it was a sound decision to employ him.

It left Paul in the wilderness. He had assumed, wrongly as it turned out, that the contract he had with Briggs Motorsport would be rolled over when the rest of the assets were bought by Triple Eight. With his additional involvement with the team in brokering the deal, it had not occurred to him that this contract could be challenged or was in any way vulnerable. The cruel irony for Paul was that he had turned down an offer from another team.

> *I had left myself wide open regarding the contract, but I had trusted those guys, and in retrospect I should have locked things down. I thought I was in business with them, but it felt like the rug was pulled out from underneath me and I had let myself be led down that path.*

There was no doubt that Paul knew that Roland Dane was a ruthless businessman — he had been warned before he joined the team. As he says, there are times when you have to have some faith, otherwise you just stand still; but he didn't realize, until it was too late, that his own contract was susceptible. He was pragmatic enough to know he couldn't compete with Craig Lowndes on merchandise lane in Australia, yet in New Zealand he was a local hero. The fans loved him, especially when he came home to race at Pukekohe, a round that was the best-attended of all V8 Supercar races outside of Adelaide. Couldn't the team capitalize on that? Greg Murphy certainly had.

He sincerely believed that he and Craig Lowndes could have worked well together, but he was to lose his drive and, it appeared, any further business association with the team, a team he had assisted into V8 Supercars. While he could rationalize the argument, he couldn't come to grips with then — or since — what seemed to him to be the apparent infidelity displayed by the very people he had helped to get where they now stood.

His only satisfaction at that time was a podium finish at Eastern Creek, after which he went to the team's headquarters to pack up his belongings. There were more than a few distraught employees in Triple Eight Racing that day; they were very sad to see him depart. He was equally gloomy. He could have chosen to insist on a fairer hearing, taken the moral high road. Indeed, he could have caused considerable havoc, but he chose not to. He worked on the principle that what is done is done: 'I grabbed my stuff, chalked it up to experience, and left.'

He did not hit back in a furious flurry of media activity, as other drivers have been known to do. Patricia, who had experience of British Touring Cars as an insider, and had knowledge of the UK personnel of Triple Eight and its management team, and who had public relations experience in the sport, was appalled and distressed. 'It pushed me too far, and I personally lost all respect for Roland, Peter and their operation.'

Ironically, Roland Dane's words of wisdom on team-building can be readily found on the www.V8X.com.au website.

Once again, Paul felt like a dowager aunt scrambling around the family looking for a home, like a Bedouin without a tent. It was the end of a season, the termination of considerable effort, a slap in the face for friendship.

At this point he hadn't considered coming home again until Murray Brown, his long-time friend and business partner from Auckland, suggested that he might like to consider it — after a fashion. There was a drive going with Team Kiwi Racing. He wouldn't have to pack up the house and transport the family elsewhere; he could stay in Australia, but in essence still be 'home' and amongst friends and family.

In taking the drive, he would replace his old friend Craig Baird. So often in the past 'Bairdo' had essentially followed Paul throughout his career: he'd won the New Zealand Grand Prix in single-seaters, he'd raced in the USA, he had gone to British Touring Cars, and had then moved into Australian V8 Supercars. This time, however, the roles were reversed.

TKR seemed like an ideal solution, even though Paul knew of the reservations many held about the franchise owner, David John. Paul thought that with all the help he had available in his own country — from family, from Murray Brown, from the media — they could make it all work. If they could all climb in and make Paul's appearance with the team work properly, everyone could benefit.

Paul put on his public relations face and did his job professionally. He was keen to do so. But behind the scenes, once more, it would be a different story.

Chapter 13

Black and blue all over

I cancelled the call in disbelief at what I was hearing. I knew at that moment I had no choice but to call it a day, and, as much as it grieved me to do so, the time had come for me to confront the situation . . .

Team Kiwi, the racing team founded by an Australian to contest the V8 Supercar Series ostensibly for and on behalf of New Zealanders, has had some of our country's most talented drivers behind the wheel. As a Kiwi brand, it has one of the largest fan bases of any team in V8 Supercars.

But something doesn't seem quite right. Around the pits it isn't hard to hear comment about David John's management methods, and he always seems to be struggling for money. In fact, it's his constant mantra.

Some of the technical team, men of many years' experience, talk of David John's interference in matters he doesn't really know a lot about, both on race day and in the workshop. Martin Collins, the softly spoken team manager, joined the team in the early days, fresh from seven highly successful years with the Lyall Williamson-run International Motorsport team that contested the

New Zealand saloon-car championships. He brought knowledge and credibility to the fledgling team. 'It was no secret,' he says, 'that David John and I fell out on a number of occasions. He couldn't hand over the reins to anyone, and in the end that's why I went elsewhere.'

Some of those who have left the team, and even one or two who remain, suggest that if David could just stick to his knitting — orchestrating sponsorship, doing some of the public duties, and taking care of basic management — all would improve. Yet anyone who pays a visit to team headquarters might see him making tea, answering telephones, tapping on a keyboard, keeping track of merchandise — doing all the things a receptionist might normally do. He is busier than a bricklayer in Baghdad, as Dick Johnson would phrase it.

The concept is a good one: a New Zealand team for New Zealand drivers competing internationally. There is nothing else in motor racing like it, and it's very similar to the way that league's Warriors, basketball's Breakers and soccer's Knights represent our country over the Ditch.

Although some serious sponsors have come on board for a time and then departed, this happens in motor sport. Nonetheless, Team Kiwi is a brand with an emotional resonance for New Zealanders and, although David John doesn't seem to believe so, there are many Kiwis who would congratulate him on starting it in the first place.

Successful Tauranga businessman and racing driver Bernie Gillon certainly thought the TKR brand had sterling qualities. Early in 2005 he met David John for the first time to discuss his potential involvement, and on 1 April that year Bernie bought 25 per cent of Team Kiwi Racing for $500,000. Part of the agreement was that this money would be used to pay off existing debt, with the surplus going into the TKR coffers. What happened over the next several months appears to indicate at best the cavalier nature of the David John school of business management and at worst a distinct lack of integrity.

Bernie was supposed to receive a disclosure of debt, but this was not forthcoming. In the meantime, Bernie paid out additional money to Paul Morris Racing in Australia (which was engineering the car) to keep TKR afloat, as David John's cashflow was precarious. This meant that Bernie's investment was increasing. Under considerable pressure, David John finally admitted that the level of debt suffered by TKR was higher than the amount he had indicated to Bernie in April. The situation was, says Bernie, a 'fiasco', and to solve the problem he suggested that he buy 50 per cent of the company and acquire half of the management responsibility. He upped his contribution to $1.2 million on the basis that the shares were to be totally unencumbered. By October 2006 he still was not officially noted as a shareholder, and at this stage he could have legally wound up Team Kiwi Racing. But he chose not to.

> *I believed in the brand and I still do. It is so important to have a Kiwi presence in V8 Supercars. We have a huge pool of talented drivers and others in the team who do a great job.*

Bernie's management experience would have been invaluable to the team, but he opted to cease direct involvement. Instead, he left his money in as a loan and allocated David John a four-month period of grace before repayment instalments needed to start. Repayment was to be spread out over three years, and in order to protect his investment Bernie took out a security over TKR assets.

While all this was going on, Paul joined Team Kiwi Racing. He had acted on the suggestion of his New Zealand marketing manager, Murray Brown, to join the 'home' team, after his unceremonious departure from driving Fords for the Triple Eight team. Murray recalls:

> *It was difficult because he was so loyal to Ford, but I'd been coming to Bathurst with Williment Sports and had seen the amount of people-support TKR got, particularly at Bathurst, Adelaide and the Gold Coast. There were Kiwis galore in phenomenal numbers and I thought it was a good brand.*

Sotto voce, he adds that the only 'unfortunate thing' was having David John at the helm. Still, Murray approached the TKR boss, pointing out he could get 'a hell of a lot worse' than Paul Radisich, and the two progressed to a deal early in 2005.

The Radisich 'brand' had considerable pulling power of its

own. Paul had a legion of fans, and he had a valuable group of commercial sponsors who had dealt with him in the past and who utterly respected his professionalism. Moreover, the media loved him, because he was always so damned co-operative. He and Greg Murphy were New Zealand's best-known drivers — their domestic profiles were probably higher than that of Scott Dixon before he won the Indianapolis 500 in May 2008.

Unfortunately, no sooner had the deal with TKR been sealed than David John announced publicly that Paul Radisich was 'expensive'. It was hardly the best or most auspicious start to their working relationship. In fact, most people involved in the sport considered that the large Australian had failed to realize what he had just obtained when Paul put his signature on the contract.

Meanwhile, back at the TKR office Murray Brown had been busy trying to get some additional sponsorship for the team, and although he talked to David John about leveraging some of TKR's existing packages, he remained suspicious about what sponsors would actually receive. In the end, Murray's nerves about how 'his' sponsors might be treated outweighed his further involvement. He basically gave up.

David John had started TKR in 2000 with a Holden, but appeared never to be fully accepted by either the Australian company or the autonomous New Zealand branch. He received some assistance from Holden New Zealand, but not nearly as much as he wanted or expected.

Nevertheless TKR started the 2005 season with what Paul rightly describes as a hiss and a roar. They were second-fastest in practice at Adelaide, third on the podium at Shanghai, and were on target for another podium finish in Darwin until a mechanical fault stopped them five laps short of the finish — all of which buoyed the team. But from there they seemed to stand still. Not all of the blame can be placed on Team Kiwi, however; Paul Morris Engineering was going through some internal turmoil as well, and this wouldn't have helped the engine development. At the same time, some of the other teams that had introduced new cars found better form as the season progressed. Paul finished the season in 14th place and headed towards 2006 hoping for better results at the start of the year by going a couple of rounds with a golfer.

New Zealand scored a most amazing sporting coup when Tiger Woods came to town. His caddy, New Zealand-born Steve Williams, occasionally races stock cars and had organized a dirt-track night at the Huntly speedway in aid of the Steve Williams Foundation, a charitable trust that benefits children. The event was timed to coincide with Steve's marriage, and it meant that Steve and Tiger could both appear at the speedway, although who knows what Tiger's sponsors must have thought of their man thrashing it out in a motor-sport event. Alongside Steve and Tiger were some men with a bit of racing experience — Paul Radisich and Greg Murphy — and one with plenty of contact sport experience, All Black captain Tana Umaga. Recalls Paul:

> *Who says golf players aren't aggressive? Tiger fired me into a concrete wall. There he was, the golfing icon of the world, and the racing was all on his terms. He was on my territory, sort of, and I more than got served by him.*

Paul cracked a rib, and today jokes that it might have been the start of his bone-breaking year . . . because along came Bathurst 2006.

Bathurst in 2006 saw Paul Radisich hospitalized and David John without both a car and a driver. It was the worst of times for everyone involved. The car was effectively a write-off, and the team had to revert to the vehicle they had used two years earlier. While Paul recuperated, TKR enlisted the services of their previous driver, Paul's good mate Craig Baird, and Fujitsu Series driver and another New Zealander, Chris Pither, to finish out the season.

The Team Kiwi boss turned pragmatic entrepreneur and organized a road show. The Bathurst-mangled Holden was towed around New Zealand, drawing fans from all over the country, who donated money to keep the Kiwi team going. The irony, of course, was that it was an Aussie going cap-in-hand to Kiwis. Nonetheless, the New Zealand public responded magnificently, donating around $350,000. We can only guess how much of that contribution was a direct result of Paul Radisich's mana.

The money raised from New Zealand, said David John, would immediately pay for a new car. Without it, he claimed, the team could not continue. The previous October, the team had sealed a deal to switch from Holden to Ford, and Ford New Zealand had approached Ford Performance Racing with the suggestion that they could engineer the Falcon for TKR.

With TKR sporting the Ford badge, Paul could return to what

many consider his spiritual home. He had raced Ford Telstars in New Zealand, and had put his signature to some limited-edition road Telstars; he had brought the Mondeo back to this country after winning the World Cup title; and had always raced Fords in V8 Supercars before joining TKR. Furthermore, Ford needed a strong Kiwi presence in V8 Supercars to combat the Greg Murphy and Jason Richards stranglehold on the New Zealand fan base, and Paul was an ideal fit.

Team Kiwi Racing thus acquired the considerable resources of Ford Performance Racing in Australia, a subsidiary of an English company owned by Prodrive, which is headed by the urbane David Richards CBE, one of the most highly respected men in the business of the sport. With that backing, Bernie Gillon's investment, and Paul's driving, David John had what appeared to be the best potential he had ever enjoyed in six years.

Still he cried hard up and the nagging suspicion that all was not well financially within Team Kiwi continued. Yet David John had Bernie Gillon's investment still available, he had sufficient money from the public of New Zealand to buy the car, he declared that all his sponsors had stuck with him, and the merchandise business, with The Rat on the T-shirts, was thriving. It's important to know, too, that FPR didn't require him to pay for the new Ford upfront. All he had to do was furnish a deposit, with the balance required within a year. It was (and still is) reasonable to ask why David John was still so short of funds after Paul's Bathurst accident.

It has been suggested that David John owed a considerable sum by the end of May 2007, but he was so consistently late with payment to FPR that a breach of agreement notice was issued.

He had scratched together part of the outstanding balance the week before by using credit cards from family members and a New Zealand broadcaster, and it was during this period that FPR received a call from a finance company in New Zealand saying that David John had put the two show cars up as security for a loan. These cars are, in fact, owned not by David John but by Ford New Zealand.

While all this was going on, Paul reduced his salary to help the Team Kiwi cause. He hadn't driven for the four months since his accident, and he knew he had to familiarize himself with the new Falcon before he could go out in anger. He advised David John he needed to do a full day's testing before he could race again.

> *To be competitive in the hardest race of the year needs a full day of testing, but unfortunately David's payments didn't come through to Ford Performance Racing and the car sat idle on the side of the track at Winton for most of the day. FPR felt sorry for me and said I could do a couple of laps. I did twenty and told David that it wasn't a full day and it wasn't fair to throw me into Adelaide.*

The official TKR line for his non-appearance was that Paul had not recuperated sufficiently. David John had always been adamant that only Kiwis would race in his cars, but given the situation he bent his own rule and hired competent young Australian Fujitsu Development champion Adam Macrow to step into the breach.

Macrow acquitted himself well, setting the seventh-fastest time in the race and finishing 16th overall, but even then David John continued to play the martyr. He issued a press release that quoted Macrow as saying 'David has copped a little flack [sic] over the decision to put me in the car . . .'

Early in June 2007, Ford Performance Racing impounded the TKR car for alleged non-payment of monies owing and called in the lawyers. David John loudly protested that he didn't owe any money, yet the prevailing motor-racing opinion considered it highly unlikely that an organization as large and respected as FPR would act impulsively and impound a car without just cause, even if David John said that's how it was.

While the two sides slugged out their legal battle, TKR did not have its tool of trade: a race car. This problem was exacerbated by the rules of the Australian V8 Supercar Series, which include a potential AU$150,000 fine for every non-appearance.

As these events were unfolding in the public arena (and there were many more machinations going on behind closed doors, too), Paul announced he was leaving Team Kiwi Racing. His press release was brief and to the point; other than saying that the terms of his contract had changed, he remained mute for the next two weeks. Perhaps predictably, David John declared Paul 'disloyal' to the New Zealand public.

Murray Deaker succinctly summed up the saga when he introduced David John to his radio show in early June 2007. 'All of it,' he said, 'has a grubby feel about it.' David John trotted out his stock-in-trade sacrificial victim act. He didn't owe FPR money, he declared; his lawyers agreed with him; he didn't know why the car had been locked up; he'll open the books; everyone's taking cheap shots; over the past five years he's taken so much crap; he doesn't live in a flash house, he lives above the workshop; the truth will out; and so on.

Two weeks after announcing his departure from TKR, Paul agreed to his first major interview. On Newstalk ZB, he said that he had enjoyed his time with TKR, where he had helped take the car from the back of the grid to the middle, to the front, and back to the back again. He wanted to continue and had thought that the money from the New Zealand public would allow that, but the terms of his contract had changed when FPR impounded the car. He wanted the public to know his loyalty wasn't in question, but what he had in front of him wasn't what he'd signed up for and so he'd made the decision to resign. When Murray Deaker asked him if the whole thing had got too messy, he simply replied yes.

I had signed a contract for another two years with TKR on the Friday before the Bathurst accident, specifically to be involved with FPR, because I knew they had a competitive car. It wasn't a loyalty issue. Dealing with David was a drama, everything was last minute and these latest things were the straw that broke the camel's back for me.

Shortly afterwards, TEGA (the entrants' organization of V8 Supercars) granted David John dispensation from the non-appearance fine at Eastern Creek. A month or so later, David John declared that the person who had handled the proceedings at Ford Performance Racing had been 'moved on', the implication being that the manager had been unceremoniously shoved aside. In fact, Rod Barrett, the commercial director with FPR to whom David John was referring, had been promoted to general manager of the overall operation, including FPR and FPV (Ford Performance Vehicles). He is a man with considerable corporate experience and is highly regarded by David Richards.

By the middle of July 2007, TKR announced a new engine supplier, concomitant team support and a new and 'exciting' young driver. Lanky Auckland teenager Shane van Gisbergen replaced Paul Radisich, and Ford Performance Racing was replaced by Stone Brothers Racing, which is owned by Tuakau-born-and-bred brothers Ross and Jimmy Stone, one of the most successful teams in Australian motor racing. It was a tangible example of the remarkable sticking power of David John, but in reality this tie-up had all the hallmarks of Ford New Zealand's efforts to prevent their considerable investment from disappearing down the gurgler.

The company had effectively ensured that David John wouldn't become unglued, even if there were plenty (in his words) who might want him to. There was also a crucial difference with van Gisbergen, who is 'owned' by Stone Brothers. All of the other TKR drivers had been 'owned' by David John during their stint with his team, but this time TKR was leasing the entire package — car, engine, development and driver.

From his home in Melbourne, Paul hinted that he was assessing a range of possible drives, maybe Europe, perhaps Le Mans; he'd

The unthinkable happened with pole position, and the unbelievable occurred with a win — the first World Touring Car Cup title at Monza, 1993. Radisich collection

A young Prince Harry accompanied by his mother, Princess Diana, visits the Ford compound at the Silverstone circuit in 1993. At Harry's request, Paul signs an autograph. Radisich collection

Team-mates, albeit briefly, in 1995. World Formula 1 and Indycar champion Nigel Mansell asked Paul for some touring-car driving tips — and then promptly went out and destroyed the car. Radisich collection

The British Touring Car Masters event, Donington, 2004. They all drove Seat Cupra R cars and proved that none of the rough-house tactics of the 1990s had diminished. Paul is left, top row. His good friend Jeff Allam is third from left, top row. Radisich collection

Learning from the master off and on the track. Paul (left) with Peter Brock at the Pukekohe round of the Nissan Mobil 500 Series, which they won, in 1989. Radisich collection

The winning Mondeo in Britain, 1993. Radisich collection

Paul and Patricia with Emilia and baby Jade at Disneyland, 2007, *en route* to spend Christmas in Britain. RADISICH COLLECTION

Paul surprised Patricia with an engagement ring in Dubai in 1997. They married the following year. RADISICH COLLECTION

The side to racing drivers the public doesn't always get to see — great Kiwi mates off the track together in Nossa, 2005. From left: Greg Murphy, Andy McElrae, Paul Radisich and Craig Baird. RADISICH COLLECTION

A third place at the Shanghai round was a portent to a future that didn't materialize, even if the fan base at the Pukekohe circuit (pictured here) is substantial and loyal. TERRY MARSHALL

Paul Radisich, Australian Glenn Seton (right) and team pictured at Pukekohe for the second round of the Nissan Mobil Series in 1993, which they won against the odds. The car had crashed heavily the week before in Wellington. Radisich collection

Back competing in New Zealand in an entire series after 15 years' racing elsewhere, at the old home circuit of Pukekohe, 2007. Euan Cameron

Three of the country's most successful single-seater drivers — and each a winner of the New Zealand Grand Prix. From left: Paul Radisich, Kenny Smith and Craig Baird, in 1991. RADISICH COLLECTION

Famous racing drivers and the girls who love them. Paul (left) with daughters Emilia and Jade, and Craig Baird with Brienna, Bathurst, 2007. RADISICH COLLECTION

The single-seater driver learns touring-car management around the streets of Wellington in 1990.
Radisich collection

All fired up in the Ford Falcon for Dick Johnson Racing, fresh from eight years in British Touring Cars.
Radisich collection

like to do some long-distance stuff, he said. At that stage, few people could imagine him landing anything close to home because all the seats appeared to be taken. Yet just two weeks later came the announcement that he had signed to drive the long-distance races with one of the prime contenders in V8 Supercars — Toll HSV — and in a Holden. Furthermore, he'd be joining his long-time mate from New Zealand, Craig Baird, who had signed earlier. If Toll HSV were to put these two Kiwis together in the same car, it would be the best New Zealand combination one could hope to have for Bathurst outside of Greg Murphy and Jason Richards. By the end of September 2007 came the announcement that that was exactly what would happen.

David John, meanwhile, announced his own driver line-up. He appointed John McIntyre to share the driving with van Gisbergen for the long-distance events, the very same driver he had vowed and declared a couple of years earlier would never, ever, be back in his team. The TKR car finished Sandown well down the field and failed to finish at Bathurst.

Paul was paired with Rick Kelly at Sandown, where they came second. The result showed that Paul had lost none of his competitive edge, but then it was highly unlikely that Toll HSV would have appointed a driver who wasn't up to the task. At Bathurst, both Toll HSV cars suffered from brake problems and neither finished.

At the start of 2008, it was announced that Shane van Gisbergen had been appointed as the second full-time V8 Supercar driver in the Stone Brothers team, alongside Australian James Courtney. This left David John scrambling around for another driver, and his press release indicated that he'd be interested in John McIntyre, one of the few full-time professional drivers in New Zealand. Johnny Mac, however, hadn't heard anything from the TKR boss, and he believes that his name may have been 'bandied around' in the press release in order to play one driver off against another. In February it was announced that Kayne Scott would replace van Gisbergen at TKR.

January had seen a flurry of other news releases. In the middle of the month, TKR announced that it was relinquishing the majority of the services of Stone Brothers Racing. The TKR board, it said, believed that the team needed more control of its own destiny, to get back to grassroots.

Bernie Gillon is convinced that the team has the potential to achieve higher placings in the championship. However, although he left some funds in the team, he withdrew his management services. He is devastated that he couldn't personally help the team achieve the goals he set. He has since bought Flamecrusher, the race-suit manufacturing company based in Tauranga. Flamecrusher provided TKR with overalls in the first year of its operation; the company wrote off the debt when they weren't paid.

Time will tell, but if there is one thing most people seem to agree on it's their surprise that David John has lasted as long as he has. One long-time observer of the sport summed up David John as follows:

If there is a fundamental difference between the majority of team owners and David John, it's that the majority of team owners find money to go motor

*racing. David John appears to go motor racing to find
money.*

Paul says he's never met anyone as resilient as the Australian.
Some would say that David John is thick-skinned, and this may
be the asset that ensures his survival. When Paul resigned from
the team he was reluctant to voice his opinion publicly, even if
other former employees of David John have not been quite so
reticent. Paul made it clear that he wanted to retain as much of
his integrity as possible.

Chapter 14

A panoramic view from the mountain

Everyone does well in that race at some point, but you can never presume you're going to win it. That's what Bathurst does to you, and it can be gut-wrenching.

Paul Radisich has contested Australia's Great Race more times than any other New Zealander in the 45-year history of the event, with the exception of Jim Richards, whose record of 32 Bathursts to date is phenomenal.

When Paul first set foot on Mt Panorama in 1988, the young Aucklander was still chasing motor sport's holy grail of Formula 1. He had raced single-seaters in his own country, and in England, America and Australia, and his mind was intent on continuing along those lines. It never occurred to him to race a 'normal' car until he got a telephone call from the Bay of Plenty.

It was pretty much a matter that I was free that weekend. There was no payment. I just said 'Yeah, I'm around', and that was the start of it.

So what if it had a tin top and wipers? All red-blooded Antipodean drivers, and more than a few from other countries, want to win at Bathurst. It's one of the world's iconic events and is widely regarded as a pinnacle of touring-car endeavour. Paul's first opportunity to take on the mountain came through Bill Bryce, a long-time supporter of motor sport.

Bill had gone to England as a circuit commentator in the 'sixties, and was thus a contemporary of Denny Hulme, Phil Kerr, Bruce McLaren and a whole host of other motor-racing people from Down Under who were established there. He became a partner in Brymon Airlines with Chris Amon, and through that was on the periphery of the Docklands development in London. He returned to New Zealand financially comfortable and bought a Lockwood Homes franchise in the Bay of Plenty.

He bought the BMW M3 that had been driven by Jim Richards and Tony Longhurst to fourth place at Bathurst in 1987, the year of the World Touring Car Championship when so many 'foreign' cars (read non-Australian) featured on the card. The second car in this JPS team had been driven by Robbie Francevic from New Zealand and a young German mechanic called Ludwig Finauer, who had come to Australia with the car as a technician. He could also pedal quite well. He had started with the BMW Motorsport Junior Team and won the Outstanding Driver of the Year award in Australia in 1986. He competed in the Amscar Series and in local touring-car races before teaming up with Robbie for the long-distance race, as a result of which he won the Bathurst Rookie of the Year award.

With the little BMW M3 still sporting JPS colours, Bill Bryce asked Paul to partner Ludwig Finauer in what was technically a

New Zealand entry. Ludwig's nickname was Goofy, as in the woof of a dog, and quite why that came about no one is sure, because he certainly isn't barking. He in turn called Bill Bryce 'Kaiser', which was apt. Bill had a little silver goatee and was known for his short fuse and his temperament, which had the tendency, when he was really riled, to turn his face a beetroot red.

Australia's Great Race was known as the Tooheys 1000 at that stage, and as Paul headed to Mt Panorama for the first time in his life he had no idea it would be the first of thousands of laps he would eventually negotiate at this track. He had heard about the circuit's fierce reputation from Frank, who had driven there in 1977 in a Mazda RX3, but even so he was remarkably undaunted.

To me, at that time Bathurst was another track, but, because it was always held up as the track in the southern hemisphere, I had some respect for it.

The BMW was fairly slow; it was very forgiving, you could do all sorts of things in it without getting into too much strife, so it was probably a great car in which to learn the track, and I managed to learn it fairly quickly.

Paul was 26 years old then, and today he has quite a different viewpoint. Admittedly he was in a much more powerful and faster car a few years later, but even so he now considers Bathurst to be one of the hardest tracks he's ever raced on. It may be the sheer number of times he's raced there — virtually every year since 1988 — and considering the number of tracks he's raced on elsewhere in the world, he's now in a position to judge.

You only get a few seconds' rest down the long straights before you have to get back over the top, and you have to concentrate so hard. Then you heave a sigh of relief because you've made it over the mountain and can get to the straights again, but it seems no time at all before once again those corners and the hill are upon you.

In any event, back in 1988 he and Finauer finished in 19th place, which wasn't bad for a little Class II effort. The race was won by Tony Longhurst and Tomas Mezera in the infinitely more powerful Sierra RS500.

Paul continued to be a busy racing driver in 1989, campaigning in New Zealand in his Swift, and hopping out of the single-seater long enough to compete in the Nissan Mobil Series, partnering Peter Brock in a Commodore and taking out first place overall. After a winter layoff, he was invited back to Bathurst for the second time, and this time he moved up a notch or three in terms of horsepower.

He was sharing a Ford Sierra Cosworth with the experienced Australian Brad Jones for the Advantage Racing Team, and had as good a shot at winning the race as anyone else on the entry list. They finished the day in ninth place in a race won by Dick Johnson and John Bowe in another Sierra. Little did Paul realize that he would be with this team in the future. Also driving a Sierra that year was the English duo of Robb Gravett and Paul's old mate from his Formula 3 days, Jeff Allam. Recalls Jeff: 'Driving for Dick Johnson was like driving for God, because he's a legend and it's a big team, but Robb Gravett was hopeless and I discovered the cars weren't that good either.'

The cars can't have been that *bad* either, because they finished in eighth place and Dick invited Jeff back for 1990. He made the long trek from his home only to discover that his little Kiwi mate would be sharing the drive with him. From the start of qualifying, their times were consistently evenly matched. Their secondary role in the two-car team was to be competitive and to be there for Shell, the sponsors. At least, that was the pre-race plan.

At just over the halfway mark, a tell-tale whistle was heard from the pits when the Boss's turbo blew and he was out of the race. Paul and Jeff, however, were leading the event. With two-thirds of the race remaining, with Jeff in the car and rain starting to fall, the team radioed through to bring him in for a pit stop. No one watching the race from the track or sitting comfortably in front of their television at home in New Zealand or Australia will forget how close this race turned out to be. Less than half a minute separated Paul and Jeff from the front-running car after nearly 1000 kilometres. They had a pit stop to come, and the DJR crew in the garage calculated that if they could get through that efficiently enough, they'd still be in the lead. As he drove into the pits, Jeff Allam was told that Dick Johnson would be replacing him in the car. He wasn't impressed.

I thought, there's no bloody way Dick's going to get into the car. I decided Paul and I were going to win

200

this race, because if Dick got into the car it would be Dick Johnson wins Bathurst and not us. So I leaned forward and bent the seat adjuster with my foot to distort the bar.

The pit stop came, and there was Dick trying to get into the seat and yelling his head off, calling us all sorts of things and waving his hands around, but he couldn't get into the car because the seat couldn't be adjusted.

Trying to move the seat back had cost them about 45 seconds longer that they couldn't afford to lose. Jeff and Paul lost the lead and ended the race in second place, 25 seconds behind the winners, Win Percy (another Pom) and the gnarled Queenslander Allan Grice, in the Chickadee Commodore. To this day Jeff Allam is adamant that they would have won the event if Dick hadn't tried to get into the car. Paul didn't know anything about the seat adjuster until after the race.

In 1991 Paul again drove for Dick Johnson at Bathurst, this time in partnership with Aussie driver Terry Shiel. They were cross-entered with John Bowe, just in case he needed to get into the car to finish the job. But he didn't. Both DJR cars failed to finish, and nowadays cross-entering isn't allowed.

Paul did not contest the 1992 Bathurst, but it was a historic event for New Zealanders for two major reasons: Denny Hulme died at the wheel of his BMW; and the race, which was shortened by rain, saw 'Godzilla' the Nissan Skyline head into the winner's circle for Jim Richards and Mark Skaife. The crowd was furious that it wasn't an Aussie car up front, and made their view known during the spraying of the champagne. Jim's famous 'you're a pack of arseholes' speech in retaliation was partly in frustration at their collective myopia and partly in response to the fact that his good friend Denny had died that day. Paul watched these scenes unfold from his home in New Zealand. It took him a long time to believe that the man who had played such a supportive role in helping him get to England to race single-seaters had passed away.

Over the next six years Paul's Bathurst races were littered with non-finishes (DNFs), although he was eighth in 1993 when he partnered Cameron McConville in an EB Falcon for Dick Johnson Racing. For two years (1995 and 1996) he didn't race there because of his commitments to British Touring Cars.

Then came the 'hiccup' years when the touring-car series cars left Bathurst and were replaced by Supertouring. In 1997 Paul got to know the man who would become his team-mate in Britain the following year. He and Tim Harvey raced a Peugeot 406, but they didn't finish. The event was won by Geoff and David Brabham in a BMW M3, after Craig Baird, who had technically won in another BMW M3, was disqualified for exceeding his allowable time in the car.

The following year, Paul raced with Paul Morris in an Audi Quattro A4, but they didn't finish either. The race was won by a Volvo S40 driven by Jim Richards and a man whom Paul had seen plenty of in British Touring Cars, the Swedish driver Rickard Rydell.

One of Paul's most memorable Bathurst drives was in 1999.

He was paired with the tall Steve Ellery in the Dick Johnson team, and although there were hopes that they could pull off a win, the reality was that Ford had won at this track only twice in the past seven years. But throughout the season they'd done a lot of development work on the new AU Falcon and a win in the last year of the 20th century would seal the new car's promise.

All through the season the AU would fall apart, the aerodynamics weren't up to much and none of the cars were competitive. The whole project had been put together badly, but when we got to Bathurst, and with the help of Dick Johnson's horsepower, the car seemed to work reasonably well on the day.

Everyone was expecting Holden to dominate, but we were leading the event, and I remember coming over the top of the mountain on the first lap and the Ford flags started waving.

As the race went on and since we were in a good position, I could see what the crowd were doing, and more and more flags were appearing. It was quite uplifting.

It didn't matter that a Kiwi was behind the wheel: the Ford fans on the mountain were excited that at long last a Ford was capable of a win. The tussle was riveting. They would be in the lead, come in for a pit stop, fall back, and then climb their way through the pack once more. Towards the end of the race, with Paul in the car and pushing hard, he came over the top of the mountain and tried to pass a slower car on the inside. They touched so lightly he didn't even feel the nudge, but it was enough to slip the valve stem out of the wheel. In an instant he had a puncture.

By the time I had climbed down the hill I couldn't turn the car into the pit lane and the shovel front dug into the road. All the dirt went into the radiator and our day was over.

They handed the win to Greg Murphy and Steven Richards, who had been chasing them all day in a Holden Commodore VT. If there was any consolation, at least the winners were New Zealanders. Another shot at Bathurst beckoned the following year, and as things turned out Paul was able to enjoy his brightest moment in a decade. His driving partner in 2000 was . . . Jason Bright.

The personable 'Brighty' had raced single-seaters in Australia with occasional touring-car drives thrown in from time to time before he headed to America to try his luck in the Indy Lights Series. He had secured a one-off Champcar drive on his home turf around the streets of Surfer's Paradise and on the strength of that, and his obvious potential as a V8 Supercar driver, Dick Johnson asked him to partner Paul in the AU Falcon at Bathurst. If both had similar early careers in single-seaters, they certainly had different likes and dislikes with the V8. 'Brighty was good and he likes a very stiff car, but that year the AU was soft and he had a bit of trouble adapting to it, but even so, he did a great job just keeping it going.'

He did indeed. And so did Paul. They finally managed a very creditable second place behind Garth Tander and Jason Bargwanna in a Holden. It had taken 10 long years of mountain climbing to achieve another podium. Steven Richards and Greg Murphy were third.

The next five years saw another clutch of non-finishes (twice with Steven Johnson, once with Max Wilson in the Betta Electrical Triple Eight Falcon, and once with Paul Morris in 2005 in a VZ Commodore), although amongst them, in 2004, Paul managed seventh place in a BA Falcon with Rickard Rydell.

Then, in 2006, came Paul Radisich's most unforgettable Bathurst of all. At Mt Panorama he had the single biggest accident of his entire career, and during the hours and weeks of convalescence he and others around him asked the same question: could this accident have been avoided? Frank had complained to the Team Kiwi Racing engineer that Paul was concerned about breaking the steering arms on what had been called 'fancy' front suspension, but Paul says that the Commodore was feeling good and that he had trust in Paul Morris Motorsport, who were engineering the car. It didn't help that the barrier he banged into was at right-angles to the track, but in the end the accident was termed a 'racing incident', albeit a tough one.

During his time in hospital, no one from AVESCO made contact with either Paul or Patricia. It was an astonishing oversight. He received a visit from the gentle V8 chaplain, Gary Coleman, and through his network of volunteers someone visited him every day, but from the organizers there was a deafening silence. Patricia was so concerned about the apparent neglect that she telephoned Wayne Cattach, the chief executive officer of AVESCO, to voice her concern. The upshot of that discussion is that, now, a procedural plan is in place so that families of injured drivers are contacted.

David John from Team Kiwi Racing never once contacted Patricia while Paul was in hospital or at home recovering.

After resigning from Team Kiwi Racing, Paul was invited, along with Craig Baird, to contest the long-distance events in 2007 for Toll HSV — one of the crack Aussie teams in the series. The call came from the team manager, Rob Crawford.

I was flattered they made the necessary changes to include me in their line-up and not only did they include me, but they unquestioningly welcomed me.

Toll HSV had signed young David Reynolds, who had won the Porsche GT3 Series in Australia, but he'd never driven at Bathurst before and the team wanted experience at this track of all places. Rather than leave David Reynolds isolated and without a drive, they orchestrated his learning experience with the Supercheap Autos team, with Cameron McConville as his co-driver.

The relationship between Paul and Craig Baird stretches back over 20 years, but they haven't always been the friends they are today. Back in the late 'eighties, when both of them were running in the Formula Atlantic series in New Zealand, they were constantly at war on the track and equally hostile to each other off it. Craig, being the younger, was the chaser who had invaded Paul's territory, and Paul was never going to gift him a win. In the maturing process, they somehow recognized this furiousness in each other and grew to develop a mutual respect far greater than either of them had ever thought they would, given their earlier history.

At Toll HSV they were made to feel at home, and the environment within the team was relaxed. Craig says that for the first time in his life he discovered at the racetrack that Paul has a well-defined sense of humour.

It took all of that time to realize he could be very funny, and it was also important that I could trust him implicitly. We never discussed it, but we both just knew and trusted each other to do the job.

Craig and Paul knew that they were driving the number-two car, and they knew the implications of that. If they were in a position to help Garth Tander and Rick Kelly, they would be expected to do the right thing as professional drivers.

In those races you work as a team and I think as you get older you can control yourself a lot better and not work so much as an individual.

For a warm-up they headed to the traditional pre-Bathurst shakedown at Melbourne's Sandown Park, where Paul was paired with one of the famous Kelly boys, Rick. They finished the Melbourne event second behind Paul's old nemesis, Craig Lowndes, who was partnered by Jamie Whincup. In a masterful piece of understatement, Paul said it sure felt good. It had been six years since he had made it to the podium in Australia, and it augured well for Bathurst. Team Kiwi Racing were the last of the finishers, in 20th.

The Rat was back, and no one in New Zealand cared that he and Craig Baird weren't in a New Zealand team. The only other time the two had driven together was at the 2002 Liquor King 500 event in Christchurch in a Falcon, and now they were in potentially one of the best cars in the field for Bathurst.

All that promise and so few brakes. Neither of the Toll HSV Commodores finished the race, but Paul was immediately signed by the team for testing and for the long-distance events for 2008. After a year of hell, a professional and personal mountain had been climbed once again.

Chapter 15

Asset deficiency and debt recovery

Here I was sitting in pole position and I was the cheapest driver in the world. The guy behind me would have been earning 20 times more than me and I had dusted him off.

In the mid-eighties New Zealand's brightest star in motor racing had been involuntarily 'resting' for about 20 months. Paul Radisich was unable to get the overseas drive he wanted because he simply didn't have the resources to do so. It wasn't through lack of trying.

More than any other sport in the world, motor racing requires a huge investment of time, money and effort, with the most important of these being money. The list of equipment that money needs to buy is formidable: tyres, a chassis, an engine, spares, tools, a trailer or transporter, a racing suit, shoes, gloves, and helmet. On top of that are race entry fees, and travel costs for the driver, several mechanics and family members. Add in the cost of race petrol, plus additional petrol if you're driving to a venue, flights if you can afford them, ferry crossings, motels and food for at least half a dozen people. There's also the ever-present potential cost of damage. All of this expense for just one weekend.

When Paul was young, his father Frank undertook the bulk of the fundraising activities, 'leaning on people' in Henderson to donate money to Paul's racing cause. After all, Frank was a local business identity. He could talk to fellow businessmen on Paul's behalf — which was just as well, because back then Paul was too shy to arrange this type of meeting. When the outcome was successful, though, he'd be sent around to pick up the cheque, which was probably good training in itself. Frank would also call on his own suppliers at the service station, negotiating *quid pro quo* deals with companies like Shell and the tyre suppliers. Local people were also in the firing line, especially the Dalmatians who owned the Henderson Valley vineyards that Paul and his brother Chris ploughed up with their motorbikes.

We'd invite as many people as possible to a barbeque at a vineyard, get everyone plastered on the cheapest local product they had available, and then have an auction and sell advertising space on the car.

These social functions were the equivalent of today's black-tie dinners at Sky City, and more than a few attendees would hide when it came to auction time. They were there for the free wine and food. Although life may have been less complicated in those days, the begging was just as ardent as it is today, and from about the age of 21 Paul was in charge of finding funds for himself. He had to learn what it takes to go door-knocking, to hustle, to coerce and try to acquire sufficient money, goods and services for the season.

The bulk of anything he raised went to supporting the core of his racing activities. Whatever was left — which typically ranged from very little to sod-all — had to pay for personal expenses. He was hardly living the high life, but by the same token he was unwittingly training himself in budget management. The more seasons he raced, the better he got at sticking to the budget and controlling expenses, and, in a sense, his own ego. He learned, for example, that he didn't necessarily need to be fast on Friday, thrashing around the track and wearing out tyres and equipment. He could save the equipment for qualifying and the race.

Even as a young man, Paul knew that he didn't want to carry on getting his hands dirty as a mechanic. What he didn't recognize at the time was that, in trying to forge a racing career, he was effectively learning to become a businessman. In fact, the only financial advice he ever received was free and obvious: no sponsorship meant he didn't race. Fortunately, he had support around him, and he and his brother worked on the project as a team. Chris kept a weather eye on the balance sheet to check on what was going out (which was considerable) and it was up to Paul to hook it back in.

His very first foray into the world of money-gathering didn't actually produce any cash. Instead, North Harbour Mazda prepared his car for the Benson & Hedges 500, in the kind of contra deal that is prevalent in motor sport. However, Paul did manage to extract a small amount of cash from Autex Industries of Avondale. The affable Scotsman running the company, Bill Cunningham, was supporting Denny Hulme and Nick Begovic in the same race and had a little left over for Paul.

The fundraising scheme that was developed in order to get Paul to England for Formula 3 for the first time was inventive and ambitious, but it didn't put money into his personal bank account. It could have, because Denny Hulme, who was helping him, donated a personal cheque to Paul. This is not the sort of thing that Denny would ever have done lightly. However, Paul never banked that cheque, because he felt that Denny had done more than enough to support his cause already.

The goal of this particular scheme was to raise £100,000, and although it didn't quite get to that level, there was just enough to get Paul into the Taylor team for six races. After that Paul came home — partly because he was broke, but partly so that he was in the right place for the future. He needed to keep race-fit so that if he did get 'the call' he'd be ready. He also needed to be able to earn enough money to survive for another season, even if that money would be spent on competing, rather than on improving his own financial situation.

I would say to myself: 'OK, I need $100,000 to do the series'. Then I'd go out and get $125,000, and put $25,000 aside towards eating and living for the year somewhere in the world. The rest would go into running the car for the Formula Atlantic championship. It kept my racing mileage up and it kept me sharp for whatever was to come up.

In between driving in New Zealand I was zipping

to the USA, where I was very much a rent-a-driver. This
enabled me to stand on the sidelines and if someone
didn't pay or was injured, I was Johnny on the spot.

When he was racing in America, Paul got a percentage of the prize money, but most of this went instantly, spent on putting a roof over his head — or more likely on trying to get his road car running. He was a racing hooker, in a manner of speaking, and it was a fairly fraught time.

The funding scheme to get Paul to England for a second shot at the British Formula 3 championship in 1986 was a clever piece of contemporary thinking on the part of Rob Whitehouse, who came up with the concept of treating Paul as an investment package for punters. However, the film producer soon found that there was a significant difference between the film world and that of professional sport. He candidly admits now that he was remarkably naïve about motor racing.

We made a very, very big mistake. Murray Taylor had
said he was owed some money by the Radisich family
and we had to pay it back. We were advised that none
of the other teams would take Paul on unless we paid
that money, but I realize now that any other team
would have snapped him up. Worse still, we paid all the
money up front! We should have paid monthly at least,
but we were relying on what we had been told.

All the frenetic money-gathering was aimed at helping Paul get a shot at Formula 1, but as we now know the 1986 season didn't go well. He had no alternative but to come back home once more to continue his single-seater endeavours. Again, it was mum and dad who supported him, although there were times when they found it hard, too, as Robyn admits:

> We'd have no money, but we'd see Paul go out there, and we knew that if he could get another set of tyres for qualifying, he would get pole. So what would Frank do? He'd go and get a new set of tyres, and even in those days it was a lot of money. Then something stupid would go wrong with the car and you'd realize you'd spent all that cash on tyres.

Despite the difficulties, Paul's burning ambition never once diminished. Neither, though, did the hard slog to find sufficient money to continue racing. Paul may have been perseverance personified, but when he came back from England after his second stint in Formula 3 he had to get a real job for the first time since his apprenticeship days at Frank's service station. In 1985, he was employed by an energy company in Hamilton, developing proposals for 'gimmicky things' they were trying to sell. He was sitting behind a desk. He had to clock in. But the urge to get back on the road and follow his passion was too great. He lasted just three months.

By around 1992, the single-seater series was in decline in New Zealand; touring cars had become more prominent, and as a result the prize money for single-seater events dropped. It cost a huge amount to compete, and the prize money was laughable. There was more promise — and better pay — in America, but even that was fraught. Still, Paul knew that if he won enough he could subsidize his New Zealand appearances. In reality, though, he was utterly reliant on friends and family for practically all of his day-to-day requirements, from food to clothing to a roof over his head.

I only did the New Zealand championship because it was the only way I had of making some money for the year, and I had to make really sure I didn't go over the budget.

Like the majority of racing drivers, Paul had to gather around him those people who could help him achieve his aims. Both of his girlfriends had acted as managers, assistants and general factotums for nothing more than glory. For a couple of seasons in New Zealand, his uncle, Tony Radisich, had provided Paul's team with a small transporter, which his girlfriend's father was able to fit out with a kitchen. Her dad was, fortuitously, in this line of business, even if the transporters he'd fitted out prior to this were horse floats. By the second year of contesting the New Zealand championship, the small transporter grew into a full-sized semi-trailer.

At this point, Paul Radisich had what aspiring young drivers and many of the general public would perceive as an extremely enviable lifestyle: he was racing at home, he was flying away overseas to compete, he was in the newspapers and on television, he had this person and that provide him with all the paraphernalia he required, he was a palpable example of a homegrown success. In truth, he was 29 years old and still didn't have any money of his own. Then out of the ether one day late in 1992, Alan Gow telephoned from England and offered Paul that lifeline. It was crunch time.

> *I had spent 12 years chasing the single-seater path, there was a lot of water under that bridge, and there had been a lot of stroking and poking people to get a chance to have a go.*
>
> *There had also been a lot of promises that didn't materialize for various reasons, so I said to myself: 'This is the time to decide whether I want to keep after that dream or whether to turn it into reality and become a professional driver and one who gets paid.'*

The offer was a good one. In the first year of driving in the British Touring Car Championship he was paid £50,000 by Andy Rouse Racing — less 50 per cent of his first year's salary, which went to Alan as a finder's fee. Paul was about to enter the best touring-car series in the world, fighting on the track amongst the world's top touring-car drivers — and he was earning no more than a competent secretary sitting behind a desk. When he claimed pole position for the first World Touring Car Cup title in Monza, the man sitting next to him in grid position number two was Nicola Larini from Italy. He would have been earning around £500,000 more than Paul.

But success breeds success, and in his second season in British Touring Cars, after 13 years of slugging it out on the track and tramping around searching for sponsors, Paul started to become financially comfortable. After his World Touring Car Cup win in Monza, he became an official Ford driver. Even then, and almost unbelievably, he negotiated his own deal with the head of Ford UK, who had telephoned Paul in his hotel room immediately after the race and asked what he wanted in a financial package.

I said I'd like a three-year contract for this amount of money and all the benefits that go with that, and he just said 'Fine' and put the phone down. I had plucked up the courage to say what I wanted and we didn't have to go through the sitting down and the talking; there was none of that, we just did it over the phone.

Paul had decided to stop being an 'Andy Rouse driver' and become a Ford works driver. He could see the benefits that brought by looking at other drivers in the series in works cars. Drivers' managers were still new to the series at that time, since most of the top drivers were well-established in the sport in England and didn't, in effect, need managing. Even so, Paul thinks it was 'bizarre' conducting the negotiations over the telephone from a hotel room, for what was the biggest deal of his life to that point. He now thinks he probably should have called on Alan Gow to help him negotiate his change of pay and circumstances with Ford. He may even have talked Gow into dropping his high commission rate.

Over the next five years, Paul's fee for racing in Britain remained healthy, thanks to the deal he had negotiated with Ford, which gave him financial credibility. Even if the car he was racing wasn't winning, he still needed to be paid a decent salary, and both West Surrey Racing and the Peugeot racing team recognized that. When he withdrew from British Touring Cars at the end of 1998 to join Dick Johnson Racing in Australia, he was comfortably off for the first time in his life as a fully professional international sportsman. It had been 19 years since he had started racing.

However, he still had to negotiate sponsorship deals for his New Zealand drives, and for that he was reliant on his Auckland-based marketing manager, Murray Brown. Over the years of their mutual involvement, Murray estimates that he has raised around NZ$2 million for the cause of The Rat. Not all that money, of course, has gone to Paul. A good deal has been used to cover the expenses involved in getting Paul to New Zealand to compete, and in the early days the majority of what was raised paid for equipment and the expenses necessary to line up on the grid.

Nowadays, there are times when Paul can command a reasonable fee and there are times when he doesn't ask for anything at all. When he stepped into the breach to drive for Garry Pedersen's team in the Liquor King 500 in 1999, replacing Mark Pedersen, who was suffering from glandular fever, he received his expenses and nothing else. He could have commanded $10,000 to $15,000 for the drive, but he didn't. It was a *pro bono* job that he undertook to give something back to the Pedersens for all the years they'd helped him out.

Paul, by accident of his birth date, was caught between an

era when natural talent was the key to the door on the road to Formula 1, and the time when money was an important prerequisite. In retrospect, he thinks he relied far too much on himself when what he really needed was a commercially constructed consortium to move him forward, very much like Scott Dixon and Brendon Hartley have employed.

The Radisich family will not say how much they have spent on Paul's racing career. In fact, it's unlikely that they've ever added it up. For them it is immaterial, because the objective was always to go motor racing and to nurture the talent of one of their own. They will not put a price on that success, in the past, the present or the future. The intrinsic value, they say, cannot be quantified.

Like the more astute professional athletes, Paul has recognized that he will need an income stream when he departs the sport, and for that reason he has shrewdly invested in property and other business interests. He is known as a canny businessman, and his brother says that he has the 'Midas touch'. He may do, but it was only after his world title in Monza in 1993 that he began to be able to diversify his financial interests and put into practice some of the lessons he had learned on the way up.

It's well documented that New Zealand's top sports broadcaster, Murray Deaker, believes that racing drivers are the easiest guests to interview by far. None of them would consider giving a monotone single-syllable answer. Even those in their teens are sufficiently media savvy to string several sentences together. One of the reasons they know how to give value back to a sponsor, suggests Deaker, is because they've been involved in the acquisition process, unlike the All Blacks, for instance.

No, Paul Radisich did not make it all the way to Formula 1, but he is still a bankable commodity, one of our top contemporary racing drivers. He is known in England, in the USA, in Australia and in other parts of the world that avidly follow his sport. He is, in that sense, truly international. There would be few who could argue he did not deserve a reasonable level of payback in the later stages of his career, especially after he endured times of near-penury for many years.

Chapter 16

Back right after this colourful message

Talking to sponsors and guests is no drama because I'm talking about something I know very well, but if I have to get up and do a speech in, say, a corporate environment, I get that sinking feeling and find it very difficult.

The stroking and poking involved in any sponsorship deal is a two-way street. There are no guarantees of a win to give a company or corporation value for its investment in the form of a front-page photo. Instead, the payback has to come in the form of value-added activity, and Paul Radisich is recognized as being very good at this.

To survive in the sport Paul learned how to promote himself at an early age, but when he made the decision to move from motocross to circuit racing, he faced a dilemma. How does an 18-year-old without a substantial portfolio of sporting success to his name convince a senior manager he is worth investing in?

The first and probably most obvious answer was to go to someone he already knew; in this case, it was to the business suppliers for Frank's service station. Mostly, the deals involved contra, in the form of product to be sold through the garage and service station. Frank did most of the talking in those days, because Paul was too inexperienced to deliver a believable spiel. However, if Paul wanted to achieve what he had set his sights on, he had no choice but to come up to speed in the market place.

He called on Ian Derbidge, a long-time PA announcer in the sport who for years had run the Rothman's hospitality unit at motor-racing events. Ian put together a professional proposal that Paul could tout around to potential sponsors. It didn't guarantee sponsorship success, but it helped make a good first impression; in those days, Paul was one of the few who thought a properly prepared portfolio was an essential tool. Even if he dreaded the cold-calling, at least he had something slick to present, and as he gained more experience at talking to marketing and advertising managers he adjusted what he wanted to achieve to suit the corporate world.

> *I realized that I could never find just one big sponsor,*
> *and that the car needed to be broken down into areas*
> *and their cost — like the nose cone, the wing, the side*
> *pods, and so on — and this worked fairly well.*

Paul was constantly on the telephone to companies to drum up support, and in 1988 he called on the head of Pioneer Equipment, Garth Hogan. The company's headline brand was VHT automotive paint, and Garth was a national drag-racing champion, so at least Paul knew he would be sympathetic to the racing cause; what he didn't know at the time was that Garth knew very little about sponsorship, despite owning and running a very successful company.

'I had sponsored various people but they were mostly mates, and none of it involved huge money. It was helping guys out with product or shipping and some cash, maybe clothing. None of them really understood sponsorship and marketing,' says Garth.

VHT's 'star' driver at the time was speedway ace Barry Butterworth, but he was of the old school when it came to taking care of sponsors. He stuck a company sign on the side of the car and that's about where it finished, even if he could generate his own publicity. He took the governing body to court over the use of his racing number, and won. 'The day after the court case, there was Barry and his car with a VHT logo on the side in a prominent position on the front page of *The New Zealand Herald.*'

It was a tangible example of the theory that any publicity is good publicity. So with VHT known to be supportive of motor racing, Paul orchestrated a meeting with Graeme Lee, the sales and marketing manager for the wholesale division.

'The next thing I knew,' recalls Garth Hogan, 'we were the primary sponsor for Paul's car, and we were spending five or six times more money on this than we'd spent on any other car. So much so that we had blown the whole marketing budget in one hit!'

Graeme Lee got a 'What the hell are you doing?' telephone call from Garth, who thought that the company was tipping the money down the drain. But as the season progressed, their involvement with Paul began to pay dividends. He won the prestigious New Zealand Grand Prix in 1988, and went on to win the majority of the races in the series to take the season title. Furthermore, the car was subsequently used by Gillette for an advertising campaign, so VHT got additional exposure without having to pay any more for it. Garth Hogan was thrilled.

For two of the three months after the racing season was finished, the Day-Glo car with VHT plastered all over it appeared on television screens every night. So as far as we were concerned, it all worked out pretty damn good.

The entire *raison d'être* for the sponsorship had thus been achieved, but, over and above that, Garth Hogan says Paul was the first person he had dealt with in sponsorship terms who was professional in his approach. He worked hard to establish relationships with those who supported him, he made himself available and, even when he had some serious international credentials on his CV, he still remembered the names of those who had aided his journey.

In 2006, Graeme Lee happened to be at the same place as Paul. Paul walked up to him and said 'Gidday'. We're talking 20 years after we sponsored him, and that typifies how professional Paul is in what he does.

Paul's money hunt never ceased, and his means of acquiring it became increasingly ambitious. In 1992, he was working on a deal to race Indy Lights in the USA in conjunction with his friend, Bob Donaldson. The plan was to ask ENZA, the New Zealand Apple and Pear Board marketing authority, to set up a travelling road show to exhibit goods and services at motor race meetings in America, with the peripheral message promoting New Zealand as a tourist destination. Reaching that number of people in the USA over one season simply couldn't be bought by any other means for the same amount of money.

It was entrepreneurial and exciting, and Paul began to wonder whether, if the proposal was accepted, he should reconsider his destination. Frank was certainly keen for him to carry on with single-seaters, and the ENZA sponsorship might be worthwhile for the UK as well. Then, at the end of the 1992 season, along came that telephone call from England with the offer to race in British Touring Cars.

I had to phone Bob Donaldson and say I was at a crossroads, because here was my opportunity to be a professional racing driver without me having to get out there and find the money. Bob was naturally disappointed because he had put a lot of effort into me driving in America, but he was good: there was no drama and he fully understood the opportunity.

ENZA was about to turn down the proposal anyway.

When Paul joined Andy Rouse in British Touring Cars he

managed to welcome Air New Zealand on board, so to speak, although it was highly unusual for the New Zealand national airline to be involved in motor racing. The company had a policy of not associating with what it saw as 'blood' sports, but Paul had successfully managed to circumvent that.

He would put on the appropriate cap for the camera and wave the banner as much as he could, but when he had an accident at Brands Hatch the airline boss wanted rid of the association. Paul had to take the logo off his helmet and not wear the cap — but he managed to keep his first-class flying concessions for a while longer.

His long association with Murray Brown, which continues to this day, began in 1989 when Paul was looking for money to contest his home series. Murray was sales manager for 89fm, a radio station that was riding high in the ratings, when Paul called in for a visit. Murray had heard of Paul Radisich, but had never met him. In fact, he wasn't particularly interested in motor racing, but, fortunately for Paul, the boss was.

Barry Everard owned 89fm and was a fan, and Murray Brown describes the sponsorship negotiations on that particular occasion as among the easiest he has ever been involved in: 'I went to Barry and straight away he said he'd give Paul $20,000, just like that, so I went back to Paul and said, "It's your lucky day, here's the cheque."'

Paul received permission from Motorsport New Zealand to use 89 as a racing number, which appeared in the shape of the radio station's logo. To leverage their involvement, 89fm took a hospitality box at the Wellington street race for the Nissan

Mobil Series. Many of those invited were from Wellington-based advertising agencies. Murray says they drank a lot of wine, ate a lot of food, enjoyed some motor racing, and the station subsequently received business from the whole exercise. In every sense the sponsorship worked well.

Around six months later, Murray Brown became Paul's professional marketing manager. In establishing this relationship, the pair set another precedent, since few drivers had ventured into this type of arrangement. They acquired Yellow Pages as a sponsor, which turned out to be the start of a long and successful symbiotic relationship. After winning the World Touring Car Cup for the second time, Paul telephoned Murray and suggested that the Ford Mondeo and the entire pit crew could be brought to New Zealand as a reward to the team and Yellow Pages.

> I said, 'Jesus, how much is that going to cost?' and he said, 'About $350,000.' I went back to Telecom Directories to see the CEO, Kevin Riley, told him how much it would cost, and asked if he would put this to the Board. I remember we were sitting in his office and he just said, 'That's fine, we're in.' I just about fell over — it meant Paul was on his way to New Zealand with the team and the Mondeo.

The association made sense. The Yellow Pages were estimated to contain around 50 per cent of motor-related advertisers, but both Paul and Murray worked at getting to know company personnel and involve them in the sport through hospitality. Many of the clients and staff who headed to the racetrack were doing so for the first time — it represented a classic example of corporate schmoozing and it was beneficial all round.

In 2001, when Liquor King pulled out of sponsoring the long-distance race they'd been involved with for two years, Murray Brown suggested that Yellow Pages could take over as principal sponsor by reshuffling the existing arrangement, in which they sponsored a two-car team. If the second car of Grant Baker and Shane McKillen could be relinquished (leaving just one car for Paul and Mark Pedersen), he reasoned, Yellow Pages would have enough money to take on the naming rights for the long-distance event. The clincher was 10 hours of television time.

There are times when the gods of sponsorship are smiling. The Yellow Pages car driven by Paul and Mark won the Yellow Pages 500. It was the perfect scenario, but it doesn't always work quite so neatly.

After he had won the World Touring Car Cup and came back to New Zealand with the Mondeo, Paul was leading the Wellington street race when he came in to the pits and handed the wheel over to Australian Glenn Seton. A few laps later and directly in front of a television camera, Seton embedded the car in the wall. The Yellow Pages sign he had slammed into was badly misshapen; the car was seriously out of shape and it sat like a wounded duck for what seemed like a lifetime in full view of every spectator at the track and thousands of television viewers around the country.

Murray Brown could see his sponsorship deal hitting the barriers as well, but between Wellington and Pukekohe the following weekend, the car was hauled to the workshop in Hamilton and repaired, and Paul and Glenn went on to win the second event. There's a corollary to this story. Two years later, when Paul and Murray were back in Wellington for a client presentation, a young man came into the pub at which the function was being hosted. He was carrying the front guard from that car. It had fallen off in the accident and he'd taken it home for posterity. Paul signed it for him.

As a result of his world title, Paul became an international sports ambassador for 'The New Zealand Way' along with Peter Blake (yachting), Mark Todd (equestrian), Phil Tataurangi (golf), and Claudia Reigler (skiing). Shot-putter Glenda Hughes and Rod McKenzie from Trade New Zealand initiated the programme in conjunction with Trade New Zealand, and the sports representatives' roles were essentially to help market New Zealand at ambassadorial and corporate functions. From time to time Paul was invited to New Zealand House in London to indulge in what he describes as social chitchat.

Many motor-sport sponsors have had their first introduction to the game through Paul, including Yellow Pages, 89fm, Ricoh, Kodak, Pit Stop, More FM, Simonize Car Care, and others. For the most part, their mutual association has worked well. What doesn't make the papers is the workload necessary to strike a deal, the door-knocking, the telephone calls and presentations that result in a dead end, neither party acquiring anything at all. In the small pond of the New Zealand sponsorship market, money is not always freely available. Often, the familiar refrain that the budget has already been spent sends the hunter back to the fray.

Murray Brown believes the successful acquisition of sponsorship can often depend on whom one approaches.

> *I like to talk to the boss, because if the boss doesn't get it, you'll never get the sponsorship. Often you'll be put in touch with the marketing manager, and even though the proposal fits perfectly with the target market, the marketing manager will put it in bin 13 before it gets to the boss and that's a toughie. I've had occasions when I've met the boss of a company I've presented to and he's said, 'Gee, if I'd seen the proposal and if I'd known it was Paul Radisich, I would have considered it.' That's a frustration.*

Some companies simply refuse to be involved in certain sports and, as a so-called 'dangerous' sport, motor racing falls readily into a no-go area for many a corporation concerned about its image, even if statistically it's not as injury-prone as rugby.

There is also an element of timing. Some years ago, Murray Brown was told by Emirates Airlines in New Zealand there were only two sports they wouldn't touch: motor racing and yachting. Soon afterwards, however, the airline was investing millions of pounds in the McLaren Racing team in Formula 1, and later Emirates became a major sponsor of New Zealand's 2007 America's Cup bid.

For all the running around involved in attracting sponsorship deals, there is some compensation besides the satisfaction of achieving targets. Before the Air New Zealand sponsorship disappeared, Paul invited Murray Brown to Britain and he flew first class.

> *It was fantastic. I put my feet up all the way, and when I arrived at Gatwick there was a new Ford Probe waiting and Paul drove me to Leamington Spa, where he lived. It was my first experience driving with him, and I held on for dear life. We were going like the clappers through these little country lanes, and I kept thinking that around the next corner there would be a harvester or something and that would be it.*

Murray went to the British Grand Prix at Silverstone, where British Touring Cars were on the undercard. He spent the day in the Ford hospitality suite and felt 'very important'. All the hours of finding funding had paid off just by being there. Paul is the first to acknowledge that they have a close relationship.

> *He's a pest! But I've never found anybody, particularly in New Zealand, who can talk about it and then follow it up like he can. To him, no means yes, or at least maybe, and he is meticulous to the point of being ridiculously painful in his job. Everything has to be followed up and dotted and teed, and he feels as if he lets himself down if these things aren't done. And as a man he has a lot of humour; he's a lot of fun and likes to have a good time and enjoys himself, and I for one enjoy Murray's company and always have done.*

Paul reckons Murray will be finding sponsorship for him until he drops dead, and even then he'll go out with a sign on the side of the casket.

Not every deal is large or involves cash, and Paul's Serengeti sunglasses were no casual purchase. The company considered that the brand association with a high-profile sportsman was the right target, even if all they could do was to remove a few items from the warehouse shelf.

If there is a distinguishing feature of the Radisich approach, it's that almost without exception sponsors he has been associated with talk of his professionalism off the track, of his willingness to become involved with the company, with staff, with media. He will sign things, make himself available for Q and A sessions, anything and everything, race schedule allowing.

They speak, too, of his thoughtfulness. When the wife of the former CEO of one sponsoring company became ill, Paul telephoned her husband and sent the woman a card. The fact that the man was no longer working for the company that had sponsored Paul was irrelevant.

It has been said that Paul learned from the public relations expert Peter Brock, yet he'd been racing around the world long before he teamed up with the Australian. Stories of his off-track politeness, his gentlemanly demeanour, his consideration towards others, had surfaced well before 1989, when he first raced with Brock. But that's not to say that he didn't absorb from the master tactician.

As a young guy, I was able to stand back to see how

Peter Brock operated, even if in the early days I was
too scared to say too much. If anything, the driving for
Peter was secondary; he had the ability to whip things
up and I was able to watch that. He was never short of
a line, he was like the Pied Piper, and he'd be there for
a long time signing autographs, and there is no doubt
he was larger than life.

Paul's approach to sponsorship may also have been influenced by two drivers who were part of the first wave of 'commercially aware' sportsmen in New Zealand. Both of these drivers had copied the American model. Steve Millen and Dave McMillan both knew how to generate a good publicity shot and how to treat sponsors professionally. They were always good copy, unlike Denny Hulme, who viewed interviews as a curse of the job — he wasn't called The Bear for nothing. Motor-sport journalist Eoin Young describes Denny telling one journalist to f*** off and come back when he had some decent questions to ask. Denny did, however, mellow somewhat in later years when he was out of the pressured environment of Formula 1. It should also be remembered that, at the time he was racing, the sport was only on the cusp of becoming a television spectacle. He hadn't grown up with the medium.

Scott Dixon, on the other hand, is thoroughly immersed in the procedure, yet he is well known as a reluctant media subject, a man of few words, if one can get to talk with him at all. He does what he needs to do and that's that. It is fair to say, though, that he has relaxed considerably since his Indy 500 win.

The best sponsorship arrangements in Paul's view are those involved with large wholesale and retail chains, which then get suppliers involved. That scenario, he says, works well for everyone, but little things sometimes mean a lot too. All those years ago when VHT were involved, numerous people would come up to him on race day to ask if VHT had Day-Glo in the paint range. If that's not a sign sponsorship is working, you'd have to ask what is.

Given his business acumen and his value-for-money approach to sponsorship, would Paul Radisich acquire his own team and take over the marketing in the future? Many of those associated with him say he'd be an ideal team boss.

The list of his attributes is formidable: he knows racing requirements, he has learned to acquire funding, he's an easy and willing interview subject with long experience in front of a camera or behind a microphone, he is running his own business away from motor racing, he has represented his country, he is comfortable conversing at high levels. Only time will tell whether he decides to take on team management — at the moment, though, he's still having fun on the track.

Chapter 17

It was bumpy there for a while

For sure you go over what happened. You definitely ask yourself questions. It's just lucky you don't come up with all the answers.

Everyone, every year, has their ups and downs, but for the most part we don't see them or their problems on television. Professional sportspeople, including racing drivers, live a lot of their life in the public domain, and we mainly see them when they are winning or when they are caught in some sort of dramatic situation.

We rarely get to know the person beneath the media persona. Most people, for instance, will have only recently learned that the triple World Formula 1 champion Sir Jackie Stewart suffered from dyslexia that wasn't diagnosed until he reached the age of 42. Perhaps only with revelations of this nature do 'stars' become more real to those of us watching from the sidelines.

Paul Radisich hadn't faced a difficulty like that. In fact, aside from having to spend so much time chasing money (and we all have to do that to some extent), he'd rarely faced any major hurdle other than the need to decide where to race, in what team, and where to live. His was a remarkably trouble-free existence in the scheme of things, especially given the nature of his chosen sport. He says of himself that he is not particularly deep, that he doesn't unduly intellectualize, and in his view this can be an advantage. He simply gets on and does. Those most close to him will tell you the same thing.

He has certainly experienced the usual disappointments, heartaches and frustrations that beset most of us, and he's turned some of those obstacles into opportunities. Breaking his back in motocross in 1980 was the first major test he faced, but out of that came circuit racing. A decade later, when he realized he wasn't going to make it to Formula 1, he wasn't short of a drive. Indeed, as it turned out, changing to a roof over his head produced some of his finest, competitively successful hours.

By the mid-to late 'nineties, with two world titles notched into his belt, he found himself trapped by a natural cycle of manufacturer devolvement in British Touring Cars, but even then he landed a professional drive at the top of the competitive tree in Australia. Over the following eight years, he had been disappointed at leaving Dick Johnson Racing, utterly gutted at being shoved aside at Triple Eight, and frustrated at Team Kiwi Racing — but none of these things, even amalgamated, added up to what Paul would term 'outside of his capacity to solve satisfactorily'.

Neither has Paul ever felt the need to bare all in public, because there was never a great deal to tell. He had put all his efforts into a professional life that was reasonably well documented. He had no reason, like John Kirwan, to admit to depression or, as in the case of Norm Hewitt, to acknowledge a problem with the bottle. Even if these things had confronted him (which they have not), he would be unlikely to discuss them outside of his immediate family. He is, essentially, a private man.

If one particular year could be categorized as an *annus horribilis* in the life of Paul Radisich and his family, however, it began in 2006, even if the origins of the problems can be traced back a little further.

Like any young couple Paul and Patricia had hoped for a family, but after a few years of marriage they realized they were having some problems achieving this goal. Although they held onto hope, every test that Patricia took proved disappointingly negative. They endured months of tests, procedures and much soul-searching, and more than once they wondered as a couple whether it was all worth it.

Around Christmas 2000, Paul and Patricia decided to halt medical intervention of the baby-production department in order to allow Paul to relax before his second season with Dick Johnson Racing cranked up again. Dick had retired from the team and was being replaced by his son, Steven, and Paul felt he had to devote more of his energies to helping the team to move forward. As sometimes happens in situations like these, nature took its course anyway.

Patricia became pregnant with their first child. The baby was due in November 2001 — except nobody told the child. Emilia

Radisich entered the world on 28 September, six weeks before the due date . . . and has exhibited doses of impatience ever since. To Emilia's credit, she waited to make her entrance into the world until Paul and Steven Johnson had won the Queensland 500 in a race that had been cut short five laps before the end by a fierce thunderstorm. After that, Paul barely had time to kiss his wife and newborn daughter goodbye before heading to Bathurst to partner Jason Bright in the AU Falcon. That was a good event, too; they were second.

Given their difficulties conceiving, and the hectic parental lifestyle that ensued because of Emilia's premature birth, they were both surprised a year or so later to discover that another child was on the way. All of the usual tests were conducted, but what followed was anything but normal. Patricia and Paul were told that their second child had Down's syndrome, a genetic disorder caused by the presence of all or part of an extra chromosome 21.

The severity of the impediment was so great that the prospect of carrying the baby to full term was limited. Even in the unlikely event of that happening, they were advised that the child would have very little chance of survival, and certainly, should the baby girl survive the birth, she would not have much quality of life. They made the very tough decision to terminate the pregnancy. 'We concluded that it would be highly selfish to bring the child into the world with those existing complications, even if the pregnancy reached full term,' explains Patricia.

It became necessary to deliver the baby over an interminable 24-hour period. They had tentatively made the decision not to see the child after the birth, knowing the full heartfelt implications if they did. But shortly afterwards and against their earlier decision, Paul asked to see and hold her. Together they said goodbye to a little girl whom they had called Hannah, from the Hebrew meaning 'grace', a child they would never get to know. It was a harrowing experience.

It would have been understandable not to try for another child, and this was discussed too, but again nature had other ideas and some four years after Emilia had been born, Patricia discovered that she was pregnant again. This time the baby went full term, and daughter number three, Jade Radisich, was born on 26 August 2005. They were enormously relieved at the arrival of a healthy, hearty baby as only parents who have experienced otherwise can fully know and understand.

Just over a year later, Paul had his Bathurst accident. It was the biggest mishap he had had in a considerably long career, and the most serious that the extended family had had to face in a lifetime of involvement in the sport. Exacerbating this already difficult situation was the knowledge that his former neighbour on the Gold Coast and fellow Kiwi, Mark Porter, had passed away the day before. Now, neither Paul nor Patricia could attend Mark's funeral, which was to be held in Hamilton less than a week later.

Paul's daughter, Emilia, had been watching the race on television. As her father was being cut free from the wreckage, she asked her mother if Daddy was dead.

Five days after the accident, when Paul was discharged from hospital, Patricia took on the role of his constant companion, preparing his medication, showering him, pushing him in his wheelchair and performing all of the tasks that he could not manage for himself, which was nearly everything. All this she did surrounded by packing boxes. It would have been far more convenient to remain in the house they had just sold, but the compensation was that the townhouse they were moving into had a pool. Obviously, they had not known when they signed up for the place that Paul would need a pool to help him heal.

Paul and Patricia, like all families involved in the peripatetic requirements of international sport, each accepted the absences that the lifestyle demands. Now, with Patricia in the role of nurse, they found themselves together constantly, and yet they were more apart emotionally than they had ever been. The experts considered this a normal consequence of Paul's accident, but in reasonably quick succession this couple had lost a child, one of their friends had been killed motor racing, Paul had had his own accident, he was seriously concerned about his potential loss of earning power and his professional direction, he couldn't manage any of his other business interests, he wasn't sure how Team Kiwi Racing would handle his absence, there wasn't any compensatory insurance coverage available, and, just to make sure they didn't have enough on their plates already, he and Patricia were moving house. Their marriage underwent a significant test period.

Paul was clearly unhappy and in physical pain. There was very little he could do but think, and for the first time in his life he began to reflect deeply as he recuperated.

I wasn't able to move, and I was uncommunicative and in my own little world. A lot of that came about because of the morphine — I was taking large doses of it, and sleeping pills, too. I tried to cut it down, but it became unbearable and I would self-medicate and then just lie there, but at the same time you know you want to get yourself out of it.

Patricia, who is one of the world's problem-solvers, felt as if she was grasping at air to bring her life back. She well knew that racing drivers are not the types to sit by the fireside smoking a pipe and patting the dog, and, no matter how much she might wish it were otherwise, Paul wasn't going to retire from the sport just yet.

Paul's physical recovery process took far longer than they had originally thought it would. The bones in his ankle were so shattered that he had to have daily physiotherapy and walk lengths in the pool in an attempt to create movement. He eventually needed a second operation to help things along. In the meantime, his head hated noise. The impact had literally rattled his brain and, although he had scans which showed there was nothing amiss there, any and every type of noise was considerably irritating.

It affected the family a lot when I was out of action. Patricia had to deal with everything on her own and the kids had to work around my injuries, and basically I was a bad-tempered bastard to be around.

He tried to push his body, based on the theory that exercising his muscles and getting everything working properly again could only aid the healing process. It didn't work like that. His body told him to stop on many occasions, and he'd have to go back to where he had left off a day or so earlier. His sternum was the first bone to heal properly, but it was six to seven weeks before he could put weight on his left leg, which was in plaster to the knee. Once the cast came off he could see some improvement, even if the deterioration in his ankle had been substantial. The second operation helped enormously.

When he came back to New Zealand in February 2007 for a promotional Team Kiwi Racing tour to show off the new Falcon, he was still hobbling. He had lost a great deal of weight and, given his normally slight-bordering-on-skinny frame, he looked decidedly gaunt. He didn't look ready to race, but he was working on his fitness regime and was confident of being physically prepared to get back into the car for the start of the new season in Adelaide in the first week of March. When he went back to Melbourne to test at Winton, he was adamant he needed a full day's testing in the car, but that didn't eventuate due to David John's failure to pay the necessary fees to Ford Performance Racing.

Although FPR relented and allowed Paul a few laps in the car, he felt underprepared and he didn't want to risk driving in the tough street event in South Australia before he was ready. However, it wasn't solely because of his physical condition that Paul decided not to race. TKR put Adam Macrow in the car.

Three weeks later, Paul returned to the track with TKR for the Perth round of the championship at Barbagallo.

It seemed like all of a sudden I was sitting there on the grid, right in the thick of things again, and I was watching the lights go green, and it hit me and I thought 'Shit'. I got off the line and then wondered if I was going to crash in the first corner. I'd had a six-month layoff and that first race was nerve-wracking.

When he got out of the car, he could barely walk; but he knew then, and only then, that he was going to get better. Back at his home track at Pukekohe in April 2007, he was given a rousing welcome by the thousands on the bank and in the grandstands. He finished 15th in the first race, 10th in the second race, and seventh in the third and final race. In the circumstances, it was a good result in front of his home crowd, but it was only a matter of weeks before he wouldn't be anywhere at all.

In June 2007 Paul resigned from Team Kiwi Racing, and by July he was wondering what the hell he could do to extract himself from the messes piling up around him. He had faced the most horrible period of his life. He was professionally, physically and personally battered and bruised. The whole family felt as if they'd been through the proverbial mill, which indeed they had.

Some of Paul's fears centred on whether he would be forced to retire before he was ready. He felt he still had some good races in him, but he also knew that at his age the offers weren't going to be thick on the ground. He hoped he might still be of use to a good team, and in early August some of his fears were assuaged when Toll HSV hired him to contest the long-distance events in Australia in a Holden Commodore.

That team certainly had faith in his abilities and, as it turned out, they were justified. On his first outing at Sandown, he and Rick Kelly were second. They would have preferred to win, of course, but for Paul it was a damn fine next-best thing, given all the physical, emotional and psychological paraphernalia that had accompanied him throughout the previous year.

A few months later, he made the decision to race in his own country with HPM Racing in the New Zealand V8 series. The team is owned by Greg Billingham and Simon Cressey, and when David Besnard vacated the seat, the owners contacted Paul. He was available, and it meant he would contest an entire domestic season in his own country for the first time since 1989.

One or two of his friends wondered quietly whether he was accepting a vastly second-best alternative and hoped privately that he wouldn't embarrass himself. In the beginning it looked as though he might. At the first round of the series at the old and familiar track of Pukekohe, he managed a creditable fourth and sixth in the first two races, but languished down in 21st place in the last race. Everyone — including every Radisich family member and every fan on the hill — hoped like hell there wasn't going to be more of the same appalling luck he'd endured the year before. They didn't have long to ponder.

At Ruapuna in Christchurch he won the round, saving his most dramatic effort for the reverse grid. He ploughed through the field like a combine harvester gobbling up chaff in spring, and captured his first individual win in a race car since driving the number 18 Falcon for Dick Johnson Racing. One of the newspapers said he showed his class. He certainly did, but little did anyone realize there was much more involved than 'merely' winning a race. To get there, Paul had overcome some significant hurdles, and in a mastery of understatement he said the win was 'kind of nice'.

Paul loves racing in his home country, and now, given he isn't in line for a full-time driving seat across the Tasman, he can. The New Zealand V8 Series is far less pressured than V8 Supercars Australia, although you might not think so if you listen to some of the snippiness from some of the top Kiwi drivers in the pits. But Paul says he's actually enjoying his sport a lot more than he has in the past decade or so; it takes him back to his early days of motor racing in New Zealand when the entire family was around him.

New Zealand racing is just as competitive as racing anywhere else in the world; there is always someone to beat, and today all the technology means that the cars are literally up to speed. It's just as professional. It's where I started, so I'm getting back to grassroots, and at the same time I'm keeping race-fit for the long-distance races in Australia and it keeps my racing miles up. In the end, though, I'm racing for my own enjoyment.

Paul and Patricia put this particularly dark period behind them and headed to England to spend Christmas 2007 with Patricia's family and with mutual friends. Paul caught up with his mate Alan Gow, his old driving partner Jeff Allam, with Dick Bennetts and Mike Ewan at West Surrey Racing, and a whole host of other people he felt at home with. Even if he didn't recognize it at the time, somewhere deep inside he needed their support.

The physical effects of his accident at Bathurst are still with him. The strengthening process, the healing, the aftermath of a workout, of driving a race car, is something he still feels, but it has improved. He says the difference between getting out of the race car at Barbagallo in 2007 and climbing out of the Toll HSV Commodore at Sandown in 2007 was about 50 per cent better and improving.

The emotional effect on both Paul and Patricia has taken its toll, too, but as a couple they are weathering the storm. More than a few of their acquaintances have remarked on the surface differences between Paul, the Westie from Henderson, and Patricia, the sedate English woman, yet in their adversity they appear to have each developed significantly more strength. Many couples could not have survived the traumas they faced over that year or more — obstacles piling up around them like an unrelenting and impenetrable stone wall.

Patricia believes strongly that they are fortunate to have the lifestyle they do and for Paul to be able to follow his passion. Paul knows it, too. When he was lying immobile after his Bathurst accident, he really wondered whether he'd ever get back in a race car.

He did and he will continue to do so.

Chapter 18

A peek inside a rat's nest

I'm not totally regimented. I definitely go along with the flow and sort of work the plan a bit on a rolling basis.

As any racing driver will tell you, it is extremely hard to make genuine friends among fellow competitors. Paul's closest mate, Alan Gow — one of the boys he allows into his personal life aside from his father — raced in Australia in his youth, and is now one of the sport's top administrators in England, heading British Touring Cars.

Alan first became acquainted with the Radisich name back in the 1970s when he was involved in Formula 5000 in Australia. At Warwick Farm circuit near Sydney, he put some money on a New Zealander no one had ever heard of who was contesting the Australian Grand Prix.

There was this guy called Frank Radisich who had rented a Matich, which at that stage was the gun car and we were having a sweepstake. I didn't know how he could drive, but with the best car the odds were good.

He didn't get his money back. The race was won by Frank Matich driving one of his own cars in his home Grand Prix, which surely must have been the better bet. But Alan Gow had been prepared to gamble, which sums up his nature.

About a decade later Alan, who by then owned a Mazda dealership in Ferntree Gully in Melbourne, was approached by Kiwi Graham Watson to help out a kid from New Zealand running in a Ralt. It was the way Wattie operated, he says — like a 'travelling bloody gypsy' — but Alan remembered the Radisich name. He tipped more money towards the second-generation racing Radisich, only this time there was a return, of sorts. He put Clemens Mazda on the side of the car, allowed the team to use his workshop, and met Paul for the first time. Alan thought he looked like a chipmunk.

He had this huge Zapata moustache under his nose and underneath were two really long front teeth. Eventually, when he could afford it and when he took more interest in his personal grooming, he had those long incisors filed down.

In 1986, it was Alan Gow who suggested that Paul could partner Peter Brock for the Nissan Mobil Series in New Zealand, thus introducing him seriously to touring cars for the first time. Among his other business interests, Alan is currently the manager of Australian driver James Courtney, who races a V8 Supercar for Stone Brothers which had been associated with Team Kiwi Racing. This places Alan — who introduced Paul to Andy Rouse —

squarely on both sides of the fence. Courtney's contract with Stone Brothers finishes at the end of the 2008 season.

Paul spent the first dozen years of his racing life either living hand-to-mouth or in low-rent flats. He boarded with Jeff Allam, his wife and their two kids in Surrey, which was much more like normal life, and he and Jeff have remained firm friends. In the USA, he stayed with friends like expatriate Kiwis Dave and Kathy White, or, when Bill Simpson was paying the bills, lived it up in five-star hotels. That was rare and only lasted from Friday night through to Monday morning, and only when he was actually racing.

He boarded with friends in New Zealand when he was racing back here, and it wasn't until he went back to England to race in British Touring Cars in 1993 that he could honestly say he was in his own home. For the first time in his life, he had to organize some furniture and conduct other normal domestic activities. It was something he'd never had to do before. He set up his first flat in Royal Leamington Spa, a town mentioned in the Domesday Book of 1086.

The picturesque town received the 'Royal prefix' from Queen Victoria in 1838 to commemorate her visit there in 1830 as a princess; in 1858 she visited again, this time as Queen. Her statue in the town still stands, although it was almost destroyed by a German bomb during the Second World War; it moved an inch on its plinth in the blast and has never been returned to its original position. The town can also lay claim to a strong sporting connection. In 1874 the modern rules of lawn tennis were drawn up at the Leamington Tennis Club; but, for motor-racing people at least, its value lies in its close proximity to the famous Silverstone circuit.

Paul's arrival in March 1993 brought him to the attention of the English woman who was to become his wife. She first saw him at the British Racing Drivers' Club hospitality suite at Silverstone: 'I noticed a younger guy I'd never seen before. I thought he was a spunk, as Australian girls would describe it, and I asked John Watson who he was.' John thought that Paul was a photographer, which seemed plausible to Patricia, but she asked Silverstone's graphic designer if that were true. He told her that Paul was a Kiwi driver taking the seat at Andy Rouse's team and his name was Radish.

Patricia had been in and around motor racing for a while and had been friendly with an Italian, even if she mostly considered racing-driver behaviour off-track as 'about kindergarten level'. Obviously, she saw something special in Paul, however, because she persevered through some slightly difficult times. After all, Patricia was public relations manager for the Peugeot team, so her relationship with Paul, who was a Ford driver, meant that she was sleeping with the enemy, and she got plenty of ribbing from the team because of it. A year or so later, Paul changed his racing steed to Peugeot, so that particular problem was solved.

Their first 'proper' home was a five-storey Regency period townhouse in a terrace of similar homes, and like a lot of the larger homes in the area it had been occupied by army officers during the Second World War. The large rooms had 3-metre-high ceilings and there was a formal drawing room on the first floor. It was a quintessentially and grandly English home, a dream home in many respects, even if the walls were a nightmare. They were partly filled with horsehair and crumbled easily.

After a few years, they moved into an Edwardian period home that had been built around the turn of the 20th century, and which again featured those large and square rooms. The living areas were spread over three floors, and the home came complete with a cavernous cellar below-stairs. Paul's favourite part of the house was the entrance hall — it was strikingly covered in black and white tiles like a chequered flag, which may have been the attraction.

In June 1997, when Paul and Patricia were on holiday in Dubai, he surprised her with an engagement ring. They planned a wedding for the following year, on 3 July 1998. The organization of the wedding was largely orchestrated by Patricia, whose event-management skills are bordering on famous. But she didn't supervise the stag night. That was organized by Alan Gow, and was staged a week before the big day. It involved taking over the entire bottom floor of a restaurant in London and decorating it in a motor-sport theme. If it was a memorable occasion for most of those who turned up, it certainly wasn't for Paul. He can't remember a thing — but for Alan and almost everyone else who had rarely seen Paul drink, it's a night they will never forget.

I was spiking his drinks, triple-strength Long Island iced teas, and I can honestly say I have never seen anyone so sick in my life as Paul. We were so concerned about him that at one stage we thought we might have to call an ambulance and take him to hospital to get his stomach pumped!

Paul's body survived the onslaught, and he and Patricia Watson married in St Mary's flint-built church in the rural setting of Wendover in Buckinghamshire, Patricia's home town, with Alan as best man. He and Paul wore Victorian frockcoats, the bride arrived at the church in a horse-drawn carriage bedecked with two chequered flags, and, as man and wife, the couple rode in this one-horsepower vehicle to the wedding reception. It was a grandly formal occasion, which Paul certainly hadn't rushed into. He was 35 years old.

Frank and Robyn were there, of course, plus Kim and her husband, Allen. For the first time in his life, Chris Radisich wore a frock coat and top hat, and he remembers standing outside the church before the ceremony and looking at some of the gravestones that dated back to the 13th century, and thinking some of those folk had been lying there for an awfully long time. A few days earlier he had been late for the wedding rehearsal because he'd been to Silverstone, also for the first time, and had stayed to look at some of the Formula 1 cars testing there. More than a few in the sport would applaud his priorities.

Nigel Arkell, Paul's team-mate from the Telstar touring car days in New Zealand, was also there, surrounded, he remembers, by a who's who of motor racing. The reception was held in what had once been a stable but was by then very much an upmarket silver-service eating establishment, and, according to some of the Kiwis, frightfully and formally English. Nigel Arkell sought to take some of the high decorum out of proceedings by shouting at the bar, but when it cost him £125 he flagged the notion after the first round.

Less than a year later, Paul and Patricia headed to the Gold Coast of Queensland. Their English homes were comfortable and reflected the well-paid lifestyle that Paul was now enjoying, and this standard could be maintained in Australia, albeit in houses with a vastly different ambience. The exchange rate certainly helped considerably.

They did what countless immigrants to Australia have done before them and headed towards the sea. Paul discovered a newly built place on Sovereign Island that had never been occupied, so they became tenants of a spacious waterfront home in one of the Gold Coast's more upmarket developments. At that stage, Paul's contract with Dick Johnson Racing was for a year and they thought that's how long they'd be staying.

There were a number of fellow New Zealanders involved in motor sport living in the area, and Paul and Patricia spent a lot of time with Craig and Louise Baird, who lived at Hope Island, a resort-style residential complex that included a golf course, a tennis centre and a supermarket. And they made new friends.

At Paul's 40th birthday party (in 2002), Louise said she looked around the room and realized she was the only person there who had been to both his 21st and his 40th.

One of the homes they rented bordered the golf course and came complete with a huge swimming pool. It was, says Patricia, like being on the set of Fantasy Island. The living was easy, the social life laidback, and they enjoyed it so much that they built their own place. Their fourth house in Queensland was Bali-inspired and was built around a central courtyard that housed two large water-features. The front door was a staggering 4 metres tall, and they say that this was their favourite home because they had both invested a considerable amount of effort into its planning.

The Gold Coast was liberally sprinkled with motor-racing Kiwis, such as Andy McElrea and his wife, Mel, who hail originally from Christchurch. There were motor-racing Aussies nearby, too. Paul Ceprnich (who was working for Paul Morris Racing), Mick and Selena Doohan, and another motorbike ace, Darryl Beattie, and his wife Laura all lived there. They had children of similar ages, and the Beattie home became the hub for parties. Steven and Bree Johnson, and Paul and Elena Morris, were already there, and as drivers changed teams other families of the racing fraternity began to arrive on the Gold Coast. Russell and Julia Ingall moved up from Melbourne, and Mark and Adrienne 'Goosie' Porter crossed the Tasman from Hamilton.

To an outsider, this type of work-together play-together group is fun, but there's a downside. The almost incestuous closeness of such a social clique can be too fragile to weather a storm, as eventually proved to be the case. The catalyst was the death of Mark Porter. A major faction split this tight-knit motor-racing community shortly afterwards, particularly among the wives. Paul and Patricia avoided most of the fall-out tension, however, because they had moved to the considerably different lifestyle of Melbourne, where Team Kiwi Racing was based.

Paul could have opted to stay in Queensland, but both he and Patricia felt that they needed a change of domestic scene; they wanted Emilia to begin her education in Victoria, a more conservative State, much colder in winter and indeed much more like England. They rented a home close to Emilia's school before buying a single-level Victorian home with a pool and a garden in Malvern. They were back to period properties after a few years of living as Queenslanders, and the house was much better suited to children. The family now included baby Jade.

This new, or old, Melbourne house wasn't to be a long-term home. In 2006, they traded their classic Victorian house for an award-winning contemporary home on the Mornington Peninsula, complete with sensational views over Port Phillip Bay and their own tennis court. When they moved to this home, Paul was still in a wheelchair.

The years of buying, redecorating and selling will continue, and maybe even increase as Paul's racing career becomes less full-time. It's what he loves to do. He's the archetypal Kiwi do-it-yourselfer, very much like his father.

At home, Paul is not one of life's early risers. He needs at least a regulation eight hours' sleep, and if he doesn't get it he doesn't function well. He likes good, healthy food, and would never indulge in the great English fry-up. He watches his weight, but if he does have a weakness, it comes in the form of chocolate. If he can't find the chocolate bars Patricia has hidden away, he will stoop to raiding his daughters' lolly jars like a seasoned criminal on a burglary spree. In this department he entirely lives up to his nickname.

Most 'normal' days, he takes Emilia to school before he heads to a regular office to run his numerous business interests, including wholesaling and retailing Australian-made carpet. He's not passionate about carpet *per se* — it's improving company performance that appeals to him. He tries to be home by 5.30pm in order to spend an hour in the gym, swimming, cycling, or all of these things. Sometimes he'll have a sauna, but the moment he gets home he is tackled by his diminutive daughters more quickly than Jerry Collins on a charge.

Not a lot of people outside the family know that Paul is a dab hand at the ironing, and is particularly good with business shirts. Yet if motor-sport fans had been listening sufficiently well when he won the first of his World Touring Car Cup titles at Monza in 1993, they would have realized the importance he places on this function. The television interviewer asked him how the win would change his life. Not much, he replied laconically, because his shirts would still need ironing in the morning.

Paul is still a tidiness freak. In fact, Jeff Allam says Paul's so tidy he's 'bloody anal'. At home he's been known to look at a messy drawer and mutter darkly under his breath 'Is this a reflection of our lives?', and from time to time he'll blitz the children's toys, sweeping them away and out of reach, which of course impresses the girls no end.

According to Patricia, however, he is to the kitchen what an alien is to earth. He relies totally on her to be fed — apart from those subversive chocolate raids — and they eat out regularly. Yet when it comes to the television remote, Paul is like practically every other man in the world, infuriatingly flicking between Foxtel channels to find motor racing, comedy or movies. He looks for the obligatory car chase or a blockbuster, and his favourite movie of all time is *Snatch*, the sequel to *Lock, Stock and Two Smoking Barrels*.

The business or professional relationship between Patricia and Paul changed when the children arrived. In years gone by, he was fully reliant on her to run his schedules, to manage his time. Now, if it's not done for him by the team, he handles his own arrangements, while Patricia continues to do the business book-keeping and runs the household. She still produces some media releases, although most teams today have entire departments or agencies handling these matters.

This couple come from different backgrounds, even if their common bond is motor racing. Patricia's family is archetypal genteel English, high tea in the afternoon and supper, not dinner. She can look pretty, proper and even a little lost in the rough-and-tumble of a large Australian motor-sport meeting, among people whose conversations start with 'mate' or 'crikey' or other more colourful introductions.

The Radisich 'team', on the other hand, is more boisterous

and down-to-earth. They gather in family and friends and envelop them in generous hospitality. They live in an old milk factory on the flat Hauraki Plains, part of which is converted into a large house. Patricia describes the family as 'big-hearted and eccentric'. Paul views his family in New Zealand (with affection) as messy, disorganized and even, at times, haphazard.

The Radisich daughters, Emilia and Jade, are far more outdoorsy girls than any little English rose, and they love the swing made out of old racing tyres that Frank has built for them. Fatherhood has certainly changed Paul. He is more openly affectionate with his daughters than he is with anyone else. He adores them, he will read to them, he will make up stories with both of them as the main characters, he plays with them, takes them swimming, to the park. He is a devoted father.

Patricia says she was initially concerned that they hadn't produced a son. Now she believes that Paul has been helped by the household's 'feminine factor'. He has no interest in exposing his daughters to anything motorized, even if Emilia has inherited genes that shows she'd be good at vehicle control and Jade comes with the supreme confidence of all three-year-olds.

Like a number of his contemporaries, Paul has a garage full of toys, some for the little children and others for the biggest child in the household. Emilia has a motorized Ferrari and a Harley Davidson model trike on which she can lean around corners with an uncommon skill. Paul has a bigger Harley, which he seldom rides, largely because of a lack of time, although it didn't stop him sending out a Christmas card one year featuring the bike, which Jeff Allam thought was 'naff'. He also owns a jet-ski, but being in Melbourne means it sees action in the summer only. There's also a kayak and a Jeep.

Paul clearly states that he owes a lot of his career success to his father and the rest of his family and to Murray Brown, and no one who knows him well can see Paul sitting in the grandstands at a race track.

He is competitive by nature; he will need to be involved somehow, in some way, and even when he does hang up his helmet, he will not languish in what could be called melancholic retirement.

Chapter 19

An update from the track

You have to do things. You have a plan and then decide where things sit in the pecking order. It's a balance between business, personal and motor-racing life as to how they pan out.

In the soporific hollow of Turua in New Zealand's North Island, a few kilometres from the almost-as-sleepy-but-larger Thames, Frank and Robyn Radisich are gearing up for another weekend of motor racing. They've been doing it for longer than they've been married. Only the names of the family participants on the track have changed.

Kim Radisich's 13-year-old is called 'AJ'. He has grown up in Turua in a house on the same large section as his grandparents'. His mother is the administration manager for Aegis Oil, the company owned and operated by her father, Frank, and so she doesn't have a great distance to walk to work.

AJ has been highly successful in motocross in exactly the same way as his Uncle Paul, who suggests, in a joking kind of way (but with a great deal of seriousness, too), that AJ should quit larking about on dirt bikes while he still has all his bones in a straight line. AJ isn't old enough to have a road licence, but he's racing a little Suzuki nonetheless, much as Scott Dixon raced a Nissan at the same age. Kim thought she could handle seeing her son racing — until it came to race day. Only then did she realize how nervous she was: 'I wanted to hide in the pits, like Dorothy Smith, but I couldn't help but watch the race.'

At Pukekohe Park Raceway in November 2007, AJ came over the hill, hit some dirt and oil deposited by other competitors and the weather, slid across the track and hit the fence. Standing together in the pits, his mother and grandmother bit their nails, closed their eyes and held their breath. AJ's Uncle Paul (who was racing at the same event in the New Zealand V8 Series) rushed over, as nervous as hell. The car was badly damaged, but AJ emerged without a scratch, just all shook up, like Elvis.

Kim and her mother exchanged one of those looks that come loaded with significant understanding. In that moment they finally knew that Paul understood what it had been like for them all those years, seeing one of their own getting into a bit of strife on the racetrack.

However, the incident didn't mean that any family member was about to stop motor racing. AJ's younger brother, Brad, is champing at the bit to get into a car himself. He's a year younger than AJ. Then there's Spence, Kim's three-year-old grandson. And grandfather Frank already has Spence's little bum on a motorbike sliding around the back yard.

As for Patricia, her ambitions are in a holding pattern until she can extract herself from being a full-time mother and wife. She wants to go to university to gain a psychology degree, in between Latin dancing and property renovations.

Paul and Patricia's two daughters are exhibiting some key family traits. Emilia is the nurturer, the peacemaker, the bookworm. Her parents, however, have no idea where her passion for singing comes from. Little Jade is curious and fearless and acts a bit like a mechanic. She gets this from Frank, they think. Both the girls love cars and bikes.

In 2007, Frank turned 70. Apart from his motor sport he also learned to fly and has owned a couple of light aircraft. There are pictures of them on the walls of the house attached to the factory. He'd still be flying and motor racing if he could, but both had to stop when he was in his late 60s, following a bizarre but serious accident at one of the rental properties Frank and Robyn own in Auckland. The tenant had telephoned about a small leak in the roof and, since the plumber who would normally fix it couldn't get there for another two weeks, Frank, in true DIY style, drove to Auckland on a showery and blustery autumn morning.

> *I put the ladder up and got on to the roof, but the wind blew the ladder down. There was no one at home except me on the roof. About 10 minutes later, the young fellow who lived across the road turned up. He was*

*about 15, so I asked him if he would come and stand
the ladder up for me. He did that and off he went. It
was windy and rainy, and I thought I had better get
down because I was going to meet Paul for lunch, so
down the ladder I went. I got halfway down and the
thing started folding on me. What the young kid had
done was put the ladder up the wrong way around
and my foot went through the aluminium rung which
started to chop the leg off below the knee. There I was,
no one about, on my own, and I couldn't get out of the
ladder no matter what I tried.*

By the time Frank arrived at Auckland Hospital, he was cold,
soaking wet and covered in blood. He was operated on by one
of the country's best-known orthopaedic surgeons, who suggested
that if Frank had not had movement in his ankle, he might not
have saved the leg. At the time, no one realized that his potentially
gloomy prognosis was a portent.

A week or so after surgery, the wound had not started to heal
and black pus oozed from the holes around the surgical 'halo'
holding Frank's leg bones together. He knew it wasn't right, but
when he picked up the telephone to talk to the doctors he had
no idea that the rampant infection that had developed could be
fatal. He was told to go to the hospital immediately, but he wasn't
quick enough. The seriousness of the situation was indicated
by the fact that the surgeon arrived before the patient. There
was no medical choice, Frank was told, but for his left leg to be
amputated below the knee.

Within weeks of having a prosthetic leg fitted, Frank was at Pukekohe racetrack for a classic-car meeting in honour of the legends of motor racing. In a remarkable example of his stoicism, he was walking with just a slight limp. It is ironic that the only significant injury he has suffered came not from motor racing, but from a ladder. Still, the Radisich patriarch will continue to work with motorbikes, with cars, with just about everything he can use a spanner on, and in the process he will teach the younger generations a thing or two.

Frank has also been heavily involved in a proposal to turn the former Air Force base at Whenuapai near Auckland into a permanent motor-sport park. The area is just a few kilometres from the Henderson Valley where the Radisich family grew up. If the motor-racing consortium is successful, Frank intends to sell Aegis Oil and concentrate on motor racing. Even if the motor-sport park doesn't happen, he might sell Aegis Oil anyway — to Paul. The lunch meeting that Paul and Frank were due to have on the day that Frank broke his leg was to discuss this very prospect.

Robyn is still feeding people at the track; she is chief cook and bottle-washer for the race team; she's the media manager; and she takes on any other spare job she gets handed. She and Frank still vociferously discuss the merits of this and that in the sport, in the team, in the world — in a healthy exchange of views which they insist on calling 'debates' and which the rest of the family would label 'arguments'. These round-table talks (which in truth can be conducted anywhere from the kitchen to the car) have been the spine of the family's togetherness for decades.

These days Paul's brother, Chris, lives in Los Angeles. He met and married an American girl and, although the marriage didn't last, his time in the USA has. He's been there for six years and is the second member of the family to have won a world motor-racing title, this one in slot-car racing, something he's been doing practically non-stop since 1970. In New Zealand, he is still recognized as a multiple winner of the New Zealand National Slot Car championships. His first race outside of New Zealand was at the International Model Car Association (IMCA) World Championships at Chicago Raceway in 1988, the same year that Paul was racing Supervee in the USA.

Chris and American Dave Gick became the world C2 endurance champions in Chicago in 1989, which earned Chris the world title. The event is genuinely international and is fiercely contested by participants from all over the world, in contrast to many 'world series' in America, in which only Americans participate. All those early years of painting his slot-cars and stinking out his bedroom in the process have paid off for Chris. He became the first member of the Radisich family to win a world title.

Today, he travels across the USA and to other countries for the sport, and is the National Director of the Slot Car Racers Association and President of the International Model Car Association. He has linked up with international slot-car racer Brian Saunders, and is in effect motor racing in a factory team. Now, where have we heard that before?

Danielle, Paul's step-sister, lives in Auckland with her husband Todd and their two children Jacob and Joshua. Not surprisingly, Todd is into cars, although he sells them, rather than races them. Nonetheless, the kids are experts on who races what, where and when, even if they don't compete themselves.

The entire Radisich family has supported Paul through many years of hard graft. His career has been their binding agent, their entire *raison d'être* and now they are doing it all again with the next generation. Their love of motor racing has come at a cost, though — personally, emotionally and financially.

There were times when Paul's racing was the sole reason for keeping the various Radisich businesses going, from the service station to the oil plant, and other sidelines in between. Other people involved in the sport have suggested that some of Paul's wider family, his Dalmatian relations, have regularly contributed to his racing coffers, but none of the immediate family is prepared to acknowledge this outright. It's a personal thing, is all they'll say.

It would be far more surprising if this hadn't happened in some way, shape or form. It is, after all, the Croatian *modus operandi familias* and has always been. The majority of Yugoslav families stick together, however many generations removed, unless they're embroiled in a vociferous factional argument, which can go on for centuries.

What of the wider circle of friends and colleagues who have supported Paul Radisich throughout his journey?

Nick Begovic has retired to the sunny climes of Northland. He still trades the occasional Porsche or BMW. He retains an interest in the car trade and can't help but do deals from time to time. It's appropriate he lives in Cable Bay, because it's by cable he receives all his motor sport coverage. He can now watch to his heart's content and when Frank and Robyn Radisich are up there as well, they all watch together. It's what they've been doing for years, whether it's standing on the side of the track or sitting together companionably on the couch.

Garry Pedersen and Mark 'Jandals' Sheehan still work together building race cars from a crowded workshop at the back of an industrial unit in Glen Eden. Mark Pedersen's Falcon in which he contests the New Zealand V8 Series is built there, along with several other cars. No doubt, in a few years' time Mark's young son Dylan will have his car worked on there, too. The matriarch of this racing dynasty is Pauline Pedersen, and like Robyn Radisich she still goes to the races to support her family, to make the lunch, to keep everything and everybody shipshape. Both women are keen for their husbands to retire, but to date neither has had much luck in that direction.

Kenny Smith, the man Paul beat in his first major single-seater appearance at Bay Park way back in 1981, is still racing. He's been at it for 50 years, and these days he races against kids more than 40 years younger than himself. He was awarded an MBE for his services to the sport — and he earned every inch of it. His family deservedly has free right-of-entry to every circuit in the country.

Graham Watson is still putting racing deals together, he's still Jonny Reid's manager, and he's still, as Alan Gow says, like a travelling bloody gypsy. But then Alan Gow likes his feet firmly plonked where they are, as managing director in charge of running British Touring Cars. He's one of British motor sport's most influential figures.

Dave McMillan lives in Indianapolis, USA, the home of the iconic Speedway. He is engineering the car of New Zealand driver Jonny Reid in the Indy Lights Series, the feeder class to the Indy Racing League, so he's still hard at it. To all intents and purposes Dave's a Yank, although he has retained a great deal of his New Zealand twang and his interest in Kiwi sport. One of the first things he does every morning is to check New Zealand websites for motor-sport information.

Dave Conti is still in the motor game and has gathered a further New Zealand connection. In 2007 he worked with young New Zealand driver Wade Cunningham in the Indy Pro Series.

The large Mr Bill Simpson from America is still manufacturing race suits, but no longer under the Simpson brand. He sold that company and started up another one called Impact, which does exactly the same thing. In 2003, he was inducted into the American Motorsport Hall of Fame.

Garth Hogan sold Pioneer Autoparts Limited and has semi-retired to Queenstown, from where he keeps an eye on what Paul is doing, because he still feels part of the team in a sense.

Rob Whitehouse now lives in Majorca. He is married with two young children and devotes his time to financing films. In 2007, his involvement included *The Good Night*, starring Penelope Cruz, Martin Freeman, Gwyneth Paltrow and Danny DeVito. He owns a Lancia Stratos, which he takes out for an airing in classic rallies now and again, film business permitting.

Andy Rouse, as we know, retired from motor racing. Mick Linford of Peugeot Racing is today more likely to be found telling British car dealers all about a new product that has just been launched than worrying about where the next penny is coming from for the track. He hasn't worked full-time since he left his official capacity with the team in the early part of this century. He enjoys it that way, because it gives him time to follow another of his passions — scuba diving.

Dick Bennetts at West Surrey Racing is still involved in British Touring Cars. In 2007, his driver, Colin Turkington, won the Independent Cup, was fifth overall in the series, and picked up a BMW corporate award at the end of the year. He, Mike Ewan and Paul Radisich have solidified their relationship.

Dick Johnson is running his own race team in the Australian V8 Supercar Series. Son Steven is at the wheel; daughter Kelly is the marketing and media manager; wife Jill is supporting the team in myriad ways, including looking after the grandchildren who come to the races. Dick finds running a team more exacting than driving. To use one of his own famous expressions, there are times when he finds himself a bit like a dog running on lino. At Eastern Creek in March 2008, Will Davison gave the team its first win in seven years, since the Queensland 500 when Paul Radisich was at the wheel. Dick Johnson said he went 'from the outhouse to the penthouse' over the win.

Roland Dane and Triple Eight are also involved in V8 Supercars. They race under the Team Vodafone banner, with drivers Craig Lowndes and Jamie Whincup sporting the same numbers once on the side of the cars driven by Max Wilson and Paul Radisich.

David John from Team Kiwi Racing is still crying hard-up and still, somehow, some way, heading proceedings.

Murray Taylor is the media manager for Brendon Hartley, who is racing for Red Bull in Formula 3 in Britain. In his spare time he is the television comments man for the Toyota Racing Series. However, some of what he knows about the sport in England and New Zealand simply can't be told on television . . .

Murray Brown works for Carnegie Sports and has an office on the Viaduct with a marvellous view of the Waitemata Harbour. Although it's a small office, it churns out big business — the company is responsible for a great deal of the signs around the major rugby grounds of New Zealand. Murray is still seeking sponsorship money for Paul Radisich when his other work commitments allow.

Some of Paul's mentors and fellow drivers are no longer here. Denny Hulme died in 1992 at Bathurst. Peter Brock died at the wheel in a rally in Australia in 2006. His influence on Paul was considerable. Paul was watching Sky TV at home when he heard that Brockie had died, and like everyone else he couldn't believe it at first. He felt sad for the loss of a friend and mentor, and also because he thought that Brockie had died at an 'inconsequential' rally. Bill Bryce passed away in New Zealand several years ago.

Whether we in New Zealand know him as 'Patch' or as 'The Rat', by any name Paul Radisich can be called an achiever. He is one of the most recognized motor-racing personalities in New Zealand. His fame is not limited to one country, however. Italians who remember Monza 1994 will never forget him, nor will the drivers at Donington Park for the second World Touring Car Cup event. Germans, Swedes and French all know, understand and appreciate his capabilities.

To put his achievements into some sort of international context, one only has to ask a London taxi driver. They are unquestionably the font of all knowledge. On four separate occasions while travelling in the back of a black cab, I was asked what I was doing in London. Every time this happened, the cabbie had heard of Paul Radisich.

To achieve that level of success in one's chosen sport, to be recognized in the street, to retain the respect and admiration of scores of people in dozens of companies over many years, to be welcomed by the media, is an enormous achievement. Paul's a lucky man. He has the kind of fortune born of sheer hard work, perseverance, family support and quite a bit of talent.

He has not retired from motor racing. Like his father, he probably never will. He is still an asset to any team, particularly in endurance racing, as Toll HSV have discovered, and he may look to Le Mans or Nürburgring or Sebring or Daytona, venues at which he would be more than capable of anchoring a team in a long-distance event.

A few years ago, Paul was asked to speak at his old school, Liston College, in Henderson. It's no longer the purely Catholic school it was when he was a foundation pupil; it has a broader base and has older pupils, as the school-leaving age has been lifted since Paul's schooldays. One of the boys asked Paul why he had left school at such a young age (15). Paul replied that he was following his dream. That was a noble pursuit, he said. If he hadn't tried to achieve it, it would have been a sin. There are three things to remember in order to be successful, Paul believes. Breathe your passion, set a goal, and persevere.

Paul Radisich, the boy from Sturgess Road in Henderson, the kid who used to tear around the Valley's vineyards on a little motorized bike and who grew to become a double world title-holder, most certainly did all these things, and much more.

In May 2008, the Waitakere City Council, which governs the Henderson Valley, recognized these qualities in Paul by impressing his footprints into granite in the Waitakere 'Walkway of Fame', which runs alongside the Civic Centre in Henderson. He joins such other inductees as sports stars Michael Jones and Beatrice Faumuina, musician Neil Finn, former Chief Justice Dame Sian Elias, and local businessman and Westie petrol-head, the late Sir Tom Clark.

Paul Radisich quite rightly stands alongside such luminaries.

Appendix

The British Touring Car Championship — who, what, when, where and why

---

We expected to come out and continue from where we had left off, but that wasn't the case — the competition had caught up.

How did Paul Radisich become a World Touring Car Cup title-holder when in New Zealand most of us didn't even realize such a thing existed? And if Europe was considered to be the international home of touring-car racing, why was Paul in a British team?

It's important to know that Paul's appointment to the Rouse team in British Touring Cars in 1993 was a case of immaculate timing for him and for the team, and that it was a key factor that led to him being recognized as one of the best touring-car drivers in the world. If he had joined the series at any other time, either before or after 1993, his world titles would probably never have happened.

To understand how British Touring Cars captured world petrolhead attention requires a history lesson.

Laying the foundations

The British Saloon Car championship had started in 1958, when it was run by the Motor Sport Association and featured separate classes for different types of saloon car. By the early 1990s, it dawned on those team owners who were mindful of television and other opportunities that the Motor Sport Association had no idea how to run a series on a more commercial footing. There was a problem, too, with an unequal class structure, which could see a reasonably underpowered car practically dawdle at the back of the field yet still pick up enough points to win the championship.

Some of the team owners sought change, and in 1992 four of them met at the workshop of Andy Rouse Engineering in Coventry to form TOCA Limited, an association of touring-car team owners. The impetus was that the licence to run the champion-ship for five years was up for renewal. Using TOCA Limited as an entity, these four team owners submitted a successful bid to become the organizers and promoters of the British Touring Car Championship. Their first task was to change the rules and format of the championship.

They introduced a 2.0-litre formula, which allowed all manufacturers to enter cars that didn't have to be homologated (have official product certification). The world governing body of motor sport (the FIA) sanctioned the series, thus engineering the demise of the horrendously expensive Group A format. The FIA shortly thereafter changed the name to Supertouring.

Introducing the original four players

The original four team owners were Andy Rouse, Dave Cook, Dave Richards and Vic Lee.

Andy Rouse was Britain's most successful touring-car driver, and he still holds the record for the most race wins by any driver in the championship's history, 60 in total. Moreover, he is a highly regarded engineer. Ford gave him the contract to build and drive the Sierra Cosworth, which dominated BTCC until the end of the decade, and in 1993, of course, he hired Paul Radisich as his team-mate in the Mondeo.

Dave Cook was a team owner running Vauxhall Cavaliers in the British Touring Car Championship, with Scotsman John Cleland and Englishman Jeff Allam as his highly competent drivers.

David Richards had come from a rally background. He was co-driver to Ari Vatanen when they won the World Rally title in 1981. He retired shortly after that and co-founded Prodrive, a motor-sport and automotive-engineering group. In British Touring Cars in 1992 he was running BMWs, with Tim Sugden and Alain Menu as the main drivers, and Kris Nissen coming in for some events. Rally star Colin McRae drove one of his cars round at Knockhill in Scotland.

Vic Lee had very successfully run Englishman Tim Harvey in the British Touring Car Championship in a BMW 318i in 1992. He was a shrewd and successful operator, but as things were to turn out, not quite shrewd or successful enough.

These four team owners appointed Australian Alan Gow to head up TOCA Limited to administer and promote the new-look British Touring Car Championship. He did not become a shareholder at this stage, because in his words he was a 'non-entity', an Australian, and he believed those running the sport were not going to hand over what he calls their crown jewels to someone they didn't know. But he is a very astute businessman.

Alan Gow had been a competitor in his own country at club-level racing. He owned a number of Melbourne-based car dealerships and had interests in commercial property. He became a partner in Peter Brock's racing team and helped to sort out Brock's tangled business life after the infamous 'energizer' issue, which saw Brock attach an 'alternative energy' device to his car, supposedly to give the engine higher performance. It became a standing joke within the racing fraternity, which eventually embarrassed Holden sufficiently to release Brock from their team. Alan was also a founder of the Australian Touring Car Entrant's Group (TEGA), which now owns and administers the Australian V8 Supercar Series.

He had taken what he thought would be a year's sabbatical from business and arrived in a wintry Britain on New Year's Eve 1990. He did nothing for about nine months, and while he was busy doing it he stayed in Allan Moffat's apartment in Knightsbridge, directly behind Harrods in fashionable Sloane Square, rent-free. Other racing drivers might express surprise at that. The Canadian-born Australian racer is believed to be extremely careful with his money, but we now know that's not entirely true. He has at least one generous bone in his body.

In addition to his landlord, Alan Gow had other connections: 'I knew Andy Rouse, because in Peter's team we had bought the Sierras off him and he co-drove for us at Bathurst. One day in

England, I phoned him up and he offered me a job.'

It was hardly surprising that the original TOCA gang-of-four wanted his expertise. He introduced television to the series, along with other marketing and promotion opportunities. Although the cars involved looked remarkably like those you might find in a home garage, the racing was hard and furious, and visually much more exciting than any championship that had preceded it. It was great viewing, both from the stands and from in front of television at home. As grid numbers increased, so did the all-important gate figures and television viewer audiences.

Gow steadily capitalized on the lot by selling packaged television coverage to other countries that by this time were starting to have their own 2.0-litre championships. It certainly helped that the iconic British television voice of Formula 1, Murray Walker, headed the commentary team.

With the building blocks laid in place, the format began to attract what David Richards calls a 'plethora' of cars and drivers, notably the Italians and the French. Britain became *the* place to go racing in Europe. There were eight manufacturers represented on the grid by 1996, with the series televised to 150 countries. No other country had anything like the sheer numbers of manufacturers participating, and the factory teams and BTCC became the biggest touring-car championship in the world. Winning a race, let alone the series, certainly earned considerable international cachet for both driver and manufacturer.

Riding the crest

To put that success into context, British football (soccer) — the country's undisputed prime sport — would regularly command crowd figures of 31,000 when, for instance, Chelsea were playing Manchester United. Yet at Brands Hatch, a British Touring Car event could command the same crowds — if not occasionally more. They weren't only petrol-heads, either; families were a feature of the audience, testament to the broad appeal of the sport.

David Richards suggests that it was due to the championship being constructed from a strong commercial base:

> *In Formula 1, you have Bernie Ecclestone with a very strong focus on the commercial activity and no one can deny the success. You see it with internal championships, like V8s in Australia, with a strong commercial emphasis, and in BTCC Alan Gow had it right.*

The *pièce de résistance* of the season brought together representatives from most of the major countries running the 2.0-litre formula, in the shape of an international one-off event: the World Touring Car Cup.

They were sunshine days, too, for the world's top touring-car drivers, who enjoyed a decent pay-packet while competing in Britain, as well as international media attention, sponsor activity, fan appreciation, and invitations to race elsewhere, particularly at Australia's Great Race, Bathurst. They might also go to New Zealand for the Nissan Mobil Series, or maybe Macau or Japan or to the International Race of Champions event in the Canary Islands.

At the end of Paul's first season with British Touring Cars, and after he'd won the first world title, Ford South Africa purchased two Rouse Sierra RS500s and invited him along for a couple of rides. He was paired with the man considered to be the Peter Brock of South African motor racing, Sarel van der Merwe.

Over there, the crowds are behind this big barbed-wire fence and they chant; they are very lively and passionate about their motor racing. I visited Sun City and got treated extremely well, and it gave us the heads-up that Vauxhall were going to be pretty competitive. I remember getting on the phone to Andy Rouse and saying the Vauxhalls were rocket ships and I don't think he believed me!

From about 1994, most of the drivers competing in British Touring Cars were paid somewhere between £200,000 and £350,000, depending on their perceived personal value. As a group, they more or less formed a cartel when it came to asking team managers for a fee, reasoning they would all lose out if one driver asked for too little, or indeed if another asked for too much. When Patrick Watts started with Peugeot in 1997 he agreed to a salary, only to be telephoned by John Cleland, who gave him a good old-fashioned bollocking for his low acceptance fee. Cleland, of course, is a Scotsman.

There were those, however, who were in a good bargaining position to ratchet up their price. Rickard Rydell, for example, received a fee at the top end of the scale, because he was Swedish, he was driving a Swedish car (Volvo), he was constantly at the front end, and his profile was high in Scandinavia. He was a bankable commodity. The same could be said of Yvan Muller from France, Jo Winkelhock from Germany, Gabriele Tarquini from Italy, and the prime example — Alain Menu, who was reportedly being paid about £600,000 around this time, plus a commission from the sponsorship he was bringing to the team. John Cleland made sure he wasn't short-changed, either.

As the seasons progressed, manufacturers were spending more and more on British Touring Cars to try to win the series. Pride was on the line, not to mention sales; the 'race on Sunday, sell on Monday' philosophy, and ego, never far away from any race track, became the driving forces. Demon tweaks adopted by one team sent every other team scurrying back to the workshop or into the protest room. Manufacturers were quick to take umbrage, and officials sometimes buckled under pressure.

To give just one example, when Alfa Romeo won the first five rounds of the 1994 season, Ford (supported by Vauxhall) complained to the race stewards about the spoiler configurations and then promptly went out to build their own, in a tit-for-tat manoeuvre. TOCA declared the Italian device illegal, and Alfa Romeo was stripped of the points they'd earned at Snetterton and Silverstone. However, the naughty-boy detention didn't last; the decision was reversed on appeal.

Other teams were facing different kinds of pressure. BMW felt continually constrained by a success penalty that applied weight. At one point, the managing director of BMW UK was so incensed at what he saw as an unfair sentence on the winning cars that he threatened to place a blow-up doll in the passenger seat at Brands Hatch to make the point that they were carrying an unwanted guest. There was even a BMW advertisement that had the drivers 'enlarged' to look like Michelin men (Bibendum) to further demonstrate the weight analogy.

There was also the matter of social standing. BMW questioned whether it was worthwhile to be beaten by (gasp!) a Vauxhall. This is simply not to be tolerated when one is positioned at the premium end of the market, you understand. BMW had moved their BTCC works cars from Prodrive to Schnitzer by this time, and this would not have come cheaply, either.

When a number of the drivers saw that the BTCC commercial operation was flourishing, they argued that they, too, should be a part of that action. TOCA had a deal with Sony to produce a PlayStation touring-car game, which became enormously popular, yet the drivers didn't receive any money for the part they played in it. Some grumbled that they had signed their potential earnings away when they put their signature to entry forms that allocated all their rights to TOCA, and some occasionally rattled the TOCA cage about the matter, but David Richards's view is clear-cut:

> *They can either take the risk with us or be paid. Most of them wanted the security of being paid and they were paid very well.*

Coming down to sea level

There is no doubt that by the late 1990s numerous manufacturers were beginning to question whether the cost of competing in

BTCC, which seemed to be getting out of hand, warranted their continued involvement, or whether they could sell cars by other, more economical, methods. To give an example: in 1990, a Vauxhall Cavalier contesting the BTCC would have had a price tag of around £60,000. By the latter part of the decade, a similar car, complete with all the sophisticated aerodynamic and telemetry systems, was costing £250,000, and for some two-car teams there wouldn't be much change out of a £10-million running budget. Inevitably, there had to be casualties, and Andy Rouse became a prime example.

When he retired from active racing, he continued as Rouse team manager for another year; but when he lost the Ford contract to West Surrey Racing, he picked up the Nissan contract, since the Japanese wanted to mount a full assault on the BTCC title in 1997. However, Nissan Motorsport Europe were unwilling to fund a full works effort and refused to pay the manufacturers' fee. Rouse was unable to score manufacturers' points as a privateer, and found himself caught between the proverbial rock and hard place.

Despite supporting BTCC for eight years and dominating their final season, Ford announced they were pulling out of the series in 2001 to focus on the World Rally Championship. They followed Volvo, Alfa Romeo, Nissan, Peugeot, BMW and Audi, leaving Vauxhall the only manufacturer to support the series with works cars. As drivers and sponsors lost interest, so did fans. The classic domino effect was in operation.

David Richards believes there is a natural cycle to manufacturer involvement in motor racing. He thinks the optimum number of manufacturers that should be involved in any series is about three, because any more means a series becomes less manageable. He is adamant that commercial and promotional activities must be conducted soundly.

There is also a natural cycle to any success, as people, fashion and circumstances change. In 2000, the original four instigators of Supertouring sold their interest in TOCA a couple of years before the MSA contract ran out. The purchaser was Octagon Motorsport, which was merrily buying up chunks of motor-sport promotion at the time, although they eventually pulled out of motor sport as they lost increasing sums of money. Their place in British Touring Cars was taken once again by the Motor Sport Association, and more than one person involved during the 1990s believes that that move heralded the decline of BTCC. It was, to all intents and purposes, back to square one.

Taking stock

Alan Gow cannily retained the licensed use of the TOCA name for video games, and in 2003 he became poacher turned gamekeeper, returning as managing director of a new company to rebuild British Touring Cars after it had floundered under the control of the previous Motor Sport Association management. He had been approached many times to come back and run the series again, and he claims it was a bit like Chinese water torture — eventually, drip, drip, drip, he gave up resisting. He declares he will never travel the same road with BTCC as before, when he was heavily reliant on manufacturers.

In 2008, the British Touring Car Championship had just two works teams, Seat and Vauxhall. The remaining nine teams are independent.

Alan Gow orchestrated a BTCC Masters Race in 2004 at Donington. There were no fewer than eight former BTCC champions in the line-up, and two former World Touring Car Cup winners (Paul Radisich and Frank Biela). They all drove Seat Cupra R championship cars owned and prepared by Seat, and if nothing else it showed the public and the competitors themselves that the rough-house tactics that permeated British Touring Cars in the 1990s had not diminished. The start grid was drawn from a hat, and Paul drew out last spot. He was also driving a Porsche Carrera Cup car that day, because, he figured, if he was going to travel that far from home to race, he may as well fill in his time constructively.

> *I was going from left-hand drive to right-hand drive and I don't think I did justice to either. I had this huge blister on my hand and I didn't have anything to put over it, and during the race it kind of blew apart. I couldn't really grasp the steering wheel that well.*
>
> *I was in the middle of the field and I missed a gear and put the thing into first! The car stood on its nose coming onto the front straight, the engine just about dropped on to the floor there and then, while the chassis wanted to keep going forwards!*

He says that it served him right for trying to do too many things at once. He finished seventh in the Seat event, in a race that was won by Anthony Reid, who beat Alain Menu by just 0.537 seconds.

Many of the top drivers of the 1990s retired or went elsewhere to race in national championships.

Will Hoy, who had driven for Andy Rouse before Paul came on the scene and who became Paul's team-mate in Ford at West Surrey Racing for one season, died of a brain tumour in 2002 at the age of 50. He had won the championship in 1991.

David Leslie died in March 2008 when the private jet in which he was a passenger crashed into a housing estate in Farnborough, Kent; fellow driver and team owner, Richard Lloyd, and data engineer, Chris Allarton, died in the same accident.

Andy Rouse spent several years trying to promote a rival series to the British Touring Car championship, modelled on the Australian V8 Supercars. The proposition didn't make it past first base, or, in motor-sport terms, past the dummy grid. He retired from any involvement in the BTCC altogether in 1996, and no longer derives an income from motor racing but is a director of his own property management company. Nonetheless, he still knows a great deal about the sport in which he made both his name and that of Paul Radisich.

David Richards has since become one of the sport's most influential figures in the complex political atmosphere of the World Rally Championship and Formula 1 management; second only, perhaps, to Bernie Ecclestone. It could be argued that his business acumen was honed during his British Touring Car days.

In 2005, David Richards was awarded a CBE for his services to motor sport. He headed Prodrive's fledgling entry into the Formula 1 World Championship for 2008, but this was scuppered by a clause in the new Concorde Agreement. Prodrive is also a partner in Ford Performance Racing, the Melbourne-based team contesting the Australian V8 Supercar series.

In mid-September 2007, David Richards and his wife were returning from a Formula 1 meeting in Belgium when he crash-landed his helicopter in North London. Both of them suffered shock. Somewhat eerily this was just two days after Colin McRae and his son (and a family friend and his son) were killed in a helicopter crash in Scotland. Richards was team boss when McRae drove for Subaru in the World Rally Championship, at the time that Possum Bourne won the Asia Pacific Rally title for that team.

Dave Cook slipped quietly away from motor racing some time around 1998, and has not retained an active interest in the sport.

Vic Lee is more remembered for his *après* race activities than his team's on-track performances, although these were not half bad. He ran top-flight drivers like Jeff Allam, Will Hoy and Tim Harvey, yet the team was beset by constant rumour and strange practice. No one could understand, for instance, why Vic Lee Racing spent so much time testing cars at Zandvoort in the Netherlands — none of the other teams went there. Constantly criss-crossing the English Channel might not have made much sense to other teams, but according to the British Police there was a great deal of method involved. In 1993 (the year Paul arrived in England to work with Andy Rouse), Vic Lee and others were convicted of importing drugs worth £6 million, hidden in their race transporters. Lee received a 12-year prison sentence. Alan Gow acquired his shareholding, with the encouragement and blessing of the others in the consortium.

When Lee emerged from 'porridge' in 2000, he merged almost seamlessly back into motor sport, running a joint campaign in BTCC and the National Saloon Car Championship, with a Peugeot 306 in each; his drivers, Toni Ruokonen and Alan Morrison, won their respective titles.

Lee ran Steve Soper and Matt Neal in the Peugeot team that Paul had vacated when he went to Australia. New Zealander Aaron Slight (who had just retired from Superbikes) was called in for one race mid-season, but in 2005 Vic Lee was again charged with drug-trafficking offences. He received another 12-year sentence and is due out around 2012.

Between his two prison stints, Lee married a woman whom Paul had got to know when he came to England, as he had stayed with her and her (then) husband, Jeff Allam. Now, like everyone else, Mrs Lee is waiting for her husband to do his time; one can only admire her tenacity. The cavernous house she and Vic once shared was requisitioned by the State to defray the expense of keeping him inside. Her circumstances are much reduced, but not to quite the extent of her husband's.

Going forward

A new World Touring Car Championship commenced in 2005 and is now arguably considered the third most important FIA championship after Formula 1 and the World Rally Championship. It is well supported by seven manufacturers and places an emphasis on curbing costs. Some of the drivers whom Paul raced against in BTCC are now contesting this series — Alain Menu, Nicola Larini, Gabriele Tarquini and Rickard Rydell, for instance.

Andy Priaulx has won the series three consecutive times.

It is unlikely a World Touring Car Cup one-off event, like those won by Paul, will eventuate in the near future, because it's simply not needed with a world series in existence. Other drivers from New Zealand may discover that chasing the single-seater dream is turning into a nightmare, and maybe turn their attention towards winning a saloon-car world championship. All they'd have to do to achieve it is show some tenacity, some talent, have their own building blocks in place, and, of course, find a considerable amount of money. But they could do it. Paul 'The Rat' Radisich has shown them how.